Young Soldiers

Why They Choose to Fight

Rachel Brett & Irma Specht

LYNNE RIENNER PUBLISHERS

Published in the United States of America in 2004 by
Lynne Rienner Publishers, Inc.
1800 30th Street, Boulder, Colorado 80301
www.rienner.com
ISBN 1-58826-285-5 (hardcover: alk. paper)
ISBN 1-58826-261-8 (pbk.: alk. paper)

and in the United Kingdom by
Lynne Rienner Publishers, Inc.
3 Henrietta Street, Covent Garden, London WC2E 8LU

Published in Switzerland in 2004 by the
International Labour Office
CH-1211 Geneva-22, Switzerland
www.ilo.org/publns
ISBN 92-2-113718-X (pbk, ILO)

Library of Congress Cataloging-in-Publication Data
Brett, Rachel.
    Young soldiers : why they choose to fight / Rachel Brett, Irma Specht.
    Includes bibliographical references and index.
    1. Child soldiers. 2. Recruiting and enlistment. 3. Child volunteers.
I. Specht, Irma. II. Title.
UB416.B74 2004
355'.00835'1—dc22   2003025740

British Cataloguing in Publication Data
A Cataloguing in Publication record for this book
is available from the British Library.

I think it is the first and perhaps last occasion that I have an opportunity to say my experience and words. . . . I thank you for coming here to record our voice and our life story.

■ Ali, *Afghanistan*

Contents

List of Photographs   xi
Foreword, Eugenia Date-Bah   xiii
Acknowledgments   xv

Introduction   1
    Vignette: Ali 6

1 The Broad Context   9
    War 9
    Poverty 14
    Education and Employment 15
    Family and Friends 23
    Politics and Ideology 27
    Specific Features of Adolescence 29
    Culture and Tradition 32
    Conclusion 36

2 The Life of the Prospective Volunteer   39
    War and Insecurity 39
    Economic Motivation 41
    Education 44
    Family and Friends 48
    The Military/Parties to the Conflict 54
    Politics and Identity 58
    Conclusion 62

3 The Critical Moment   65
Outbreak of Violence *65*
Lack of Income/Poverty *66*
School *67*
Family Events *68*
Friends *71*
Recruitment *71*
Conclusion *73*
Vignette: Sayanathen *75*

4 A Complex of Risk Factors   77
Javad's Story *77*
Identifying Risk Factors and Their Linkages *79*
Conclusion *82*

5 Girls and Boys   85
Religion and Ethnicity *87*
Domestic Exploitation and Abuse *88*
Societal Expectations and Roles *91*
Protection for Self and Family *93*
Education *96*
Reaction to Involvement *97*
Demobilization and Reintegration *98*
Conclusion *100*

6 The Concept of Volunteering   105
Volunteering for What? *105*
How Voluntary Is Voluntary? *108*
Legal Issues *112*
Conclusion *117*

7 Conclusion   121
Key Factors *123*
The Right to Leave *128*
Improving Socioeconomic Reintegration *129*
What Prospects? *135*

Appendix 1: Research and Methodological Issues   137
The Project Proposal *137*
The Case Studies *139*
Selection of Informants *142*

The Methodology of Data Collection *143*
The Primary Data *144*
Analysis and Interpretation of Data *147*
Instructions Provided to Researchers *149*

Appendix 2: Conflict Profiles   163
Afghanistan *163*
Colombia *165*
Republic of Congo (Congo-Brazzaville) *167*
Democratic Republic of Congo (DRC) *169*
Northern Ireland *171*
Sierra Leone *173*
South Africa *175*
Sri Lanka *177*

Bibliography   179
Index   186
About the Book   192

Photographs

An abandoned tank serves as a playground   10

Schools are used to promote recruitment to the armed forces   20

Friends from childhood often join the same outfit together   26

Artwork created by former young soldiers portrays
    scenes of war   34

Many join because there are no other options   42

Violent heroes (such as Che Guevara) have a strong
    influence   55

For many children, violence is just around the corner   57

War is part of the normal everyday environment   67

Girls are also involved in active combat   94

Young soldiers look upon the realities of war   111

Education and employment opportunities mitigate
    adolescents' need to "volunteer"   130

Foreword

T he world is currently witnessing a grave trend in the form of more than 300,000 children actively involved in armed conflicts.

With the adoption, in 1999, of the Convention on the Worst Forms of Child Labour, No. 182, the International Labour Organization (ILO) was called upon to contribute to international efforts to prevent and end children's participation in armed conflicts, one of the worst forms of child labor. The Convention, now ratified by 136 ILO member states, calls inter alia for the urgent elimination of forced recruitment of children in armed conflicts.

This book brings together the children's own views about why they are combatants. It highlights a number of the factors contributing to their joining up, including the nature of their socioeconomic environment, vulnerable personal circumstances and triggers, and how these diverse risk factors interact. In the process, it also draws attention to the gender dimensions of the problem. Additionally, it examines the question of how "voluntary" the young soldiers' participation really is, and whether this difficult choice should ever be presented to a child.

Many of the conditions described by these young soldiers relate to forced labor. They live in fear for their lives, not from the enemy but from their own units; they are often not paid; their working conditions are quite different from what they expected; and they are unable to flee from their predicament. Here again, the accumulated experience of the ILO in applying the Forced Labour Convention, No. 29 (1930), can be invaluable in helping actors address these many issues.

This book highlights a number of the key factors to be considered in a serious comprehensive strategy to tackle the problem. They include the need to take into account the root causes—the changed nature of weapons and warfare, the breakdown of law and order, and intolerable levels of poverty, unemployment, inequality, and other forms of social exclusion, as well as weaknesses in the educational and vocational training systems, rampant violence and abuse meted out to children, and social pressures on children to engage in armed conflicts and other of the worst forms of child labor. The strategy should also include intensified efforts to prevent and resolve the numerous armed conflicts around the world.

By focusing on the real stories of the young soldiers themselves, the book provides a valuable addition to existing materials for advocacy, policy, and action against this heinous trend.

Finally, the ILO's Crisis Response and Reconstruction Programme expresses its gratitude to Rachel Brett and Irma Specht, the authors of this volume, as well as to all the consultants and ILO and non-ILO personnel who contributed to the data collection and analysis for the book. Above all, our special thanks go to the young soldiers for sharing their painful personal stories with us.

—*Eugenia Date-Bah*
Director, InFocus Programme on
    Crisis Response and Reconstruction,
International Labour Organization

Acknowledgments

This book is the result of a collaborative process involving not only the authors, but also the researchers—Hanne Beirens, D.G. Harendra da Silva, Nematallah Fazeli, Marie-Eliane Kombo, Arshad Mehmood, Katy Radford, Feyi Rodway, Amanda Romero, Ibrahim Sesay, and Jawad Ullah—and all those who worked with them. Tim Bogaert, Derek Brett, Rebecca Kmentt, and a series of interns—Annemiek Buskens, Emily Slater, Rachel Taylor, and Catherine Ukelo—edited and provided additional materials. In addition, of course, we thank the young people who were interviewed, without whose cooperation the book would not have been possible.

The authors owe a debt to their families for their patience, support, and assistance—Korak, Farai, Lucky, and Marcel Specht; Lydia Aarsman-Verhoef and Peggy, Edward, and Jennifer Brett—and to friends and colleagues Stephen Ellis, Jayasankar Krishnamurty, Muqtada Muhammed, and Wouter van Beek for suggestions, encouragement, and proposed revisions.

The comments of the external reviewers, Paul Richards and Gerrie Ter Haar, and those of our colleagues from the International Labour Organization's International Programme on the Elimination of Child Labour (IFP/IPEC)—Anita Amorim, Francesco D'Ovidio, Joost Kooijmans, Yoshie Noguchi, and Tine Staermose—were invaluable, and the persistent and patient support of Eva Tanner (Quaker United Nations Office, Geneva) and Rosemary Beattie, Charlotte Beauchamp, Lauren Elsaesser, and Jesica Seacor (ILO Bureau of Publications) was essential.

The authors are especially grateful to Marcel Crozet for coordinating and facilitating the collection of visual material, as well as to the photographers themselves for helping the book to "speak": Georges

Cabrera, Marcel Crozet, Pascal Deloche, Armin Linke, Martin Lueders, Enric Marti, Dominic Sansoni, and Teun Voeten.

Finally, the authors would like to thank the Ministry of Foreign Affairs of the Kingdom of the Netherlands for funding the Voices of Young Soldiers Research Project, and the ILO InFocus Programme on Crisis Response and Reconstruction (IFP/CRISIS) and the Quaker United Nations Office, Geneva, for investing extensive staff time in this project.

Introduction

*What people believe as a motive for their conduct is at least as
important as the actual sequence of events.*
> ▪ Stephen Ellis, *The Masks of Anarchy*

Children are among the fighters in most of today's armed conflicts.
International attention has been given predominantly to those who have
been abducted or physically forced to join, particularly those in the
lower age ranges. This is not the whole story. Thousands more join
armed forces or armed groups apparently through choice. A recent study
by the International Labour Organization (ILO) found that "volunteers"
accounted for two-thirds of child soldiers interviewed in four Central
African countries.[1] Under-18s are routinely recruited into national
armies and armed groups in many countries throughout the world.

The aim of this book is to give a better insight into the realities of
these young "volunteers." Through in-depth interviews with young soldiers and ex-soldiers from around the world who classify themselves as
having volunteered for armed service, we consider the situation from
their perspective. Listening to what they say may help in understanding
what drives or leads them to join up.

There are a number of assumptions challenged through the experiences of these young people, one of the most fundamental of which is
the voluntary nature of the decision to join up. Equally controversial is
the questioning of the assumption that the situation of Western young
soldiers differs in all respects from non-Western, and that the experience of those joining the regular army is necessarily dissimilar from
that of young people joining armed groups. It is hoped that giving these
young people the chance to speak out and bringing their diverse voices

together will invite a more honest look at the common reasons for young people joining armed forces or groups, and will take the understanding of these issues a step further. This in turn will give greater insight into the difficulties in demobilizing and reintegrating ex-soldiers, and the particularities of girl soldiers in this context, and thus assist local, national, regional, and international actors to respond better to them.

The 53 boys and girls interviewed for this research project had all been involved with armed forces or armed groups before they reached the age of 18 years. They were part of national armies, paramilitaries, rebel groups, or other armed groups. In order to ensure that differing circumstances and cultures were taken into account, a variety of situations were selected. At the same time, the nature of the research project required that the young people be accessible for interviews in circumstances that would not put them at additional risk—which is also why the names used for all the interviewees are fictitious—and where suitably qualified "local" interviewers were available. (Appendix 1 gives a full explanation of the research project and the methodology used.) It is in the nature of qualitative research that both the number of situations covered and the size of the sample in each are small; all conclusions are, therefore, tentative. For this research, young people were interviewed from 10 situations: Afghanistan (refugees in the Islamic Republic of Iran), Colombia, the Republic of Congo (referred to here as Congo-Brazzaville, and formerly known as Middle Congo), the Democratic Republic of Congo (DRC, formerly known as Zaire), Pakistan, Sierra Leone, South Africa, Sri Lanka, and two separate situations in the United Kingdom: young people associated with paramilitary groups in Northern Ireland[2] and young members of the British armed forces.[3]

The authors pass no judgment on the merits of the decision to join made by the young people, the reasons given, nor, indeed, on the factual accuracy of the accounts; nor do they take any political position on the conflicts themselves (a short description of each of which can be found in Appendix 2). Our purpose is to understand how things look from the perspective of the young soldiers themselves. The particular choice of these very different sociocultural and economic national contexts reflects the global nature of the problem, but this diversity may also throw into relief the similarities that exist between the voices of these young soldiers.

Because the subjects of the study were adolescents, they are not referred to here as "children" although under international law all persons under the age of 18 years are so classified. The focus on adolescents must be stressed. This age group accounts for the vast majority of the world's "child soldiers," yet was identified by Graça Machel in the *UN Study on the Impact of Armed Conflict on Children*[4] as being the most neglected age group.[5] Adolescents are in transition from childhood to adulthood. There are certain things that impinge more directly on them than on adults, such as education or the lack of it. There are other things to which this age group is more prone than are younger children, such as the forced sexual experiences of adolescent girls. Adolescence is a time of vulnerability with the uncertainties and turbulence of physical, mental and emotional development. It is also a time of opportunities with greater freedom, developing understanding of one's own identity and place in the community and society, and a new capacity to make choices and to take on responsibilities. The stage of puberty, during which many of these young people joined, is characterized by feelings of opposition and resistance to authority and power structures in the family, at school, and at state level. In addition, it is a time when injustice and its unacceptability are strongly felt. The reasons why young people join armed forces and armed groups reflect all these aspects of their specific stage of life.

Much of the explanation of why young people are drawn into armed conflict can be found in shared features of their environment, and parallels can be traced across the differences between countries, cultures, and types of conflict. Previous research on child soldiers has identified a number of key factors for child participation as well as which categories of children are most at risk.[6] In particular, those who become child soldiers have been found to be overwhelmingly from the poor and disadvantaged sectors of society, from the conflict zones themselves, and from those with disrupted or nonexistent families. The present study confirms these earlier findings, but goes further in analyzing and interpreting *why* this is the case and the complexity of how these and other factors relate to and interact with each other in real life. Such an approach from the "inside" rather than the "outside" has rarely been featured in the literature until now.

What the present research identifies is that there are not only various factors that lead to involvement—always, of course, in combination—but also that these factors operate at different levels. Asked what leads to child participation in conflicts in Africa, those working in the field usually reply, "poverty."[7] It is indeed true that most child soldiers come from impoverished circumstances, and not only in Africa. However, many poor children do not become child soldiers. Thus it is clear that although poverty may create a general vulnerability to military recruitment, it cannot be the only factor.

Such general environmental factors set the context without which involvement is highly unlikely to happen. There is a second level of factors, however, relating to the individual's personal history, which predisposes certain young people to join the army or the conflict, while others who share the same general environment do not. Indeed the precise combination of factors that lead in each individual case to this decision is unique. Even then it is not decisive. In each individual story there is a third level: there is a trigger for the specific decision to join up. What is it that tips the balance from thinking about it to taking the decision and acting on it? Some young people think about joining for years before actually doing so. Obviously many who do not join also think about the possibility, but the particular combination of factors does not occur, or there are countervailing ones. By contrast, some have not considered it at all until their world disintegrates and they see no other option. Many of the same factors that set the scene or are part of the more specific situation of the young person are often the ones that crystallize into a particular moment of decision.

Across these three different levels, the same types or categories of reason can be seen to apply in different ways and to different degrees. These can be divided into the broad areas of war, poverty, education and employment, family and friends, politics and ideology, specific features of adolescence, and culture and tradition. This is demonstrated and explored through the testimonies of the young people themselves in the first three chapters of the book.[8]

The linkages between the three levels of environmental factors are explored in Chapter 4. However, as this book is based on and primarily concerned with in-depth interviews with young soldiers and ex-soldiers, it does not pretend to take account of every theory or possible factor for their involvement. There are almost certainly additional features that do not emerge here. It is nonetheless important to recognize that some of the conventional wisdom related to this subject may represent adult perceptions from the outside rather than the reality experienced by the young people themselves.

In the course of this research, some interesting differences emerged between the reasons for joining given by girls and those given by boys. A preliminary attempt is made in Chapter 5 to identify and comment on these, while recognizing that the exceptionally small size of the sample requires that any conclusions be treated with extreme caution.

Although all these young people defined themselves as having volunteered rather than being forced to join, the analysis of the factors that led to their involvement nevertheless raises questions about the effective degree of free choice in many cases. Specific attention to this aspect is given in Chapter 6, within the context of the international debate on the subject.

Even from the limited statistical information available,[9] it is clear that the majority of those recruited under the age of 18 remain involved in the military or armed conflict well into adulthood, although some do extricate themselves and others are captured. For those being demobilized and reintegrated while still young, it is wrong to assume that this necessarily takes place following the end of the conflict. In many situations such programs operate against a backdrop of unstable circumstances or even continuing conflict. (Armies do not normally demobilize their soldiers during the conflict; this is a feature peculiar to the issue of *child* soldiers, arising from local, national, regional, and international pressure.) Particularly in such situations, when the young people were not abducted or physically forced to join in the first place, the demobilization and reintegration are unlikely to be successful or sustained unless the reasons why they became involved are addressed. Even if they temporarily return to civilian life, they are likely to be drawn back into the conflict.

It is essential, therefore, to understand the reasons that they themselves identify for joining armed forces or armed groups, whether by individual choice or as the result of other factors. In turn, understanding why they joined indicates what needs to be done if others are not to follow in their footsteps. As some of these young soldiers themselves recognize, joining not only has the immediate consequences of their participation in the conflict, but also forecloses other future possibilities even when (or if) the conflict ends. Chapter 7 addresses this directly by bringing together conclusions and recommendations for policymakers and workers in the field.

This book is a tribute to the young people who shared their stories and reflections. Their strength of character, courage, commitment, and tenacity deserve recognition. It is also a memorial for their friends and the many others who did not live to tell their stories.

Vignette: Ali, now 20, is from Afghanistan but living in the Islamic Republic of Iran[10]

When I was about 7 or 8 years old and I was in class 7 and I was living in a Mojahedin war zone, I was a good schoolboy and my literacy was so good. When I was going to school I simultaneously worked in a medical clinic belonging to Médecins sans Frontières [MSF]. Our school time was 8 to 12 in the morning, and in the afternoon we were free, so I went to the medical clinic of the French doctors. There I began to learn first aid such as injection, dressing of a wound, and so on, and I became a first aid helper with the Mojahedin; I always worked to support the Mojahedin. That time I did support and worked as medical helper behind the strongholds. I gradually learned some advanced medical skills. When I was 12 and 13, I attended in surgical operation room and I did work as a surgical assistant. When my knowledge developed and after a few months MSF held some medical courses to teach medicine helping, surgery, and general medicine, and I took part. So now I am familiar with many medical and surgical skills. For instance, I know orthopedics and I can bone-set whenever needed.

When I was 10 years old a war began between Esmail Khan, the commander and governor of Herat, and the state forces, meaning Dr. Najibollah's cabinet. Because our area had a strategically very crucial position, Dr. Najibollah's forces surrounded the area for about 10 months and 7 days. We were fighting all the time, and 560 people of the Mojahedin and about 1,700 of the state forces were killed and injured.

I was among Esmail Khan's forces. I became familiar with different war weapons and guns such as the Kalashnikov. After 5 or 6 months' fighting, I had to return to the hospital. I was just a 10-year-old boy but the only one who was familiar with medicine in the area. When the area became a war zone for some reason, all doctors and nurses left the place. When the French medical group left Afghanistan, I ran the clinic, because there was no doctor and nurse, there was no one to help the injured soldiers.

Later, when we were fighting the Taliban, sometimes our forces captured an injured enemy soldier. I treated the injured soldier of the Taliban group in the same way that I treated our own soldiers. I didn't discriminate between him and our soldiers. He appreciated me. Later, when the Taliban was in power, I was captured and imprisoned by the Taliban again. When I was in prison, that injured Taliban soldier who I treated saw me by accident. He was a commander and released me.

Because my average of exams was very high I was allowed to attend the university entrance examination in Afghanistan. And I did. I successfully passed the exam and was accepted to study medicine. I studied some medical courses, but due to having a very bad war experience I no longer like medicine. I saw too many injured people and I don't like to deal with patients and wounded people. I haven't got a diploma. I was injured several times as well. Now I have difficulties with my eyes. I suffer from cataracts and pearl-white. Before attending in the war I was hale and hearty. Because I dealt with injured soldiers, now I have some blood diseases as well. I have hepatitis and my blood is polluted with hepatitis.

Notes

1. According to ILO research, two-thirds of child soldiers interviewed in Burundi, Congo-Brazzaville, the Democratic Republic of Congo (DRC), and Rwanda said that they took the initiative of enrolling themselves "voluntarily" (Dumas and de Cock 2003, p. viii).

2. Regrettably, despite the best efforts of the research team concerned, it did not prove possible to obtain interviews with those young people associated with Republican paramilitary groups, because of the sensitive situation in relation to the cease-fire.

3. The latter was included because of the large numbers of 16- and 17-year-old volunteers recruited each year: 7,676 in 1999 (Coalition to Stop the Use of Child Soldiers 2001). Until 1 September 2002, under-18s were routinely deployed into combat. Permission was given to interview some of their "satisfied soldiers": those who have volunteered to spend a year working in recruitment centers.

4. Machel 1996.

5. This judgment was reiterated by the Women's Commission for Refugee Women and Children, 2000, p. 1: "Adolescents are in desperate need of increased attention by the international community."

6. See, in particular, Brett and McCallin 1998 and Machel 2001.

7. See, for example, McConnan and Uppard 2001, p. xx: "Poverty is a major factor in the recruitment of children."

8. Some of the transcripts are reproduced in translation or in the words of the interpreter; others reproduce the English of the interviewee (with some editing for literacy and readability). See the section on linguistic differences in Annex I for a discussion of this issue.

9. Brett and McCallin 1998; Coalition to Stop the Use of Child Soldiers 2001 and 2002.

10. For general background information, see the Afghanistan conflict profile in Appendix 2.

1

The Broad Context

Trying to analyze human behavior and identify the specific factors or incidents that lead to one course of action rather than another is inevitably a complex and somewhat unsatisfactory process. Few things in life are so clear-cut that there is one single explanation for them; an individual may give several explanations for a particular action or omission for this very reason. Moreover, different aspects of a story will take on importance with each telling, and the perspective of the listener may be different again.

The testimonies of the young people who took part in this study are complex and diverse, but their voices weave together to give a picture of some of the underlying and immediate causes for their joining an armed force or armed group. This book attempts to draw from these causes a framework of factors that may put a young person at risk of military involvement.

This first chapter identifies the significant environmental factors that are, as it were, the sine qua non—the necessary but not sufficient conditions—without which adolescents are highly unlikely to join up. These environmental factors can be divided into seven broad categories, which are dealt with in turn: war, poverty, education and employment, family and friends, politics and ideology, specific features of adolescence, and culture and tradition. Many of the same issues come up again but with greater specificity in the personal situation of the young people (Chapter 2) and at the moment that the young person actually makes the decision to join (Chapter 3).

War

Most of the young people who become involved in warfare do so because there is a war. This is so obvious that too little consideration has been given to war itself as a causal factor in their involvement.[1] (The term "war" is used throughout this book as a general shorthand to cover situations of international and internal armed conflicts, and also situations of militarized violence that may not amount to armed conflict in the strict legal sense.)

War creates the environment for child soldiering in different ways. First, for young people war rapidly becomes the normal everyday background to their lives. Second, the war comes to them, rather than them going to look for a war to fight. Third, living in a violent situation creates the need for self-protection and to use violence to do so. Fourth, war is the cause of many of the other conditions, such as the closing of schools, exacerbated social tensions, family breakup, and increased poverty, which can also contribute to their involvement. Finally, although many children play at war games, watch war movies, and dream of the adventure and heroism of war, only some are in a position to actually try it out. Thus war is not only an environmental factor in its own right, and a root of many of the other causes that push or pull young people into participation, but also provides the opportunity.

The long-running nature of many of today's conflicts—whether permanent or sporadic—means that for large numbers of children and

Photo by M. Lueders

An abandoned tank serves as a playground

young people war is the normality rather than the exception. Adults may have a concept of a different time when life was peaceful and "normal" and thus that war is an aberration. Many children are born into the war and have never known anything else or, if they did, peace was for them no more normal than war.

I knew of the war from the time I was a small child. I knew the world of war only. • Ajith, *Sri Lanka*[2]

Aye. There's always been trouble, like . . . Since I would have known it. It's actually calmed down a bit now. • Paul, *Northern Ireland*[3]

Throughout our history, Afghans have always carried weapons. It is because of security problems. In Afghanistan there was only the town or the central cities that had police and commanders to keep and save the citizens, but out of the cities people had to save themselves by themselves. So, they carry guns and weapons, and in some rural areas people have had military groups to guard the people. Usually the young people have been members of these guardian groups.
• Hassan, *Afghanistan*

They [guerrillas] were always passing by there, by the house.
• Alfredo, *Colombia*[4]

Even when there is no current armed conflict, the normality of the military environment may be a factor:

I was brought up with the army. My dad used to be in the Engineers. So all my life, I'd been on pad estates [army housing estates], living with the army, basically. [. . .] I just took it as normal.
• Andrew, *United Kingdom*

In most cases, the young people do not go out to find a war to join. The war is all around them, or comes to them:

I entered in war very early, when I was about 12 or less. [. . .] I came to Mazarsharif for schooling and I became involved in war. I never wanted to use a gun and I never wanted to fight in my country. [. . .] We had to defend and fight, there was no way but war.
• Hassan, *Afghanistan*

When the war broke out, we fled in the villages, but over there, there were loads of Ninjas, then if you don't want to get killed, well, you become Ninja. Then when you succeeded in running away, you cut your hair off and then you returned to Brazza, but there the problem is exactly the same; if you don't become Cobra, well one will kill you, then you become Cobra, because you don't have another choice. If you don't want, you'll get killed because they will say that you're an infiltrator. ▪ Pierre, *Congo-Brazzaville*[5,6]

Yes, they [the guerrillas] were there every day. I mean, at least when I was living there. I mean, when I joined them, they were there [. . .] amongst the houses, you could say, because they were right there, they had a little camp not far away. ▪ Jessica, *Colombia*

Well, when they [the Armed Forces Revolutionary Council (AFRC)] entered into Kono, [. . .] when they entered our location, the only way to be free was by living with them. I was expecting that after that time things will be easy for me, but that was not the way things worked. They permanently lived with us. ▪ Arthur, *Sierra Leone*[7]

You have to join one or the other, because most down here, like, they're either in one organization or the other.

▪ Billy, *Northern Ireland*

Although there are individual exceptions:

Though I planned to join the combat, we went there as tourists, just like people go for trips to Murree for recreation, that's why we left for Afghanistan.[8] ▪ Muhammad, *Pakistan*[9]

Living in a context of armed violence influences young people to use armed violence themselves. It creates feelings of insecurity, and an atmosphere in which violent behavior is considered legitimate and is linked to the ready availability of weapons:

You see, like all the people there, it's like: they defend themselves with knives, and so, why not me? I'll do the same and we won't let anyone try and pull a fast one on us. ▪ Richard, *Colombia*

I just know it's an organization that's going about to try and clear this place up and doesn't let things go bad about the Shankill Estate, because the Ulster Freedom Fighters has it all organized, and they have ways that if there's joy riders, or people who sniff glue, they would be punished for it. They wouldn't let you do it. Things like that. ▪ Michael, *Northern Ireland*

It also leads to the need for self-protection:

> *Because in the war, the civilians are maltreated. When you are a*
> *civilian in the war, it's hard.* ▪ Germain, *DRC*[10]

> *Congo is a turbulent country, violence is often around us [. . .] there*
> *are often settling of scores, and in order to protect yourself you have*
> *to fight.* ▪ Albert, *Congo-Brazzaville*

For girls there are particular aspects in addition to the general violence
of warfare:

> *It's because of the war. When it's the war, you don't choose. . . .*
> *Because if you have weapons, you can defend yourself, if you don't*
> *have any, you are beaten, one kills you, and one rapes you, even the*
> *boys.* ▪ Christine, *DRC*

War leads to the availability of guns and familiarity with them:

> *All groups began to import military weapons to the country. After*
> *a few months every corner of the country became full of guns and*
> *weapons. So, it was very easy to become familiar with guns. Instead*
> *of toys we had lots of weapons.* ▪ Hassan, *Afghanistan*

> *I saw my cousin with guns. When he was looking after them, once I*
> *took one of those guns out, without permission. When you're young,*
> *you are very curious about these things, to see them fire it and*
> *everything.* ▪ Andrés, *Colombia*

War disrupts the family and other social support networks. It dis-
places families, in the short or long term, and disperses their members,
leaving adolescents to fend for themselves, or to provide for and protect
younger siblings. Conflict may also aggravate social tensions between
generations and racial, ethnic, and religious groups. It leads to the closure of schools and destroys the social and economic infrastructure.

Although war creates many problems, it also provides opportunities. For those seeking an escape from home, whether escape from
abuse or exploitation or as an act of rebellion, or merely seeking adventure, the possibilities and the temptations are different if you are in a
war or warlike situation. The obvious and most readily-available escape
route will be into the army or an armed group. This is, inevitably, true
particularly for those individuals or categories with the most limited

alternative options: girls, those without money or the means of livelihood, and those with little or no education.

Poverty

Like war, poverty is a major environmental factor making children and
young people vulnerable to involvement in armed forces and armed
groups.[11] It is perhaps the most obvious common feature of child soldiers generally, which is one of the reasons why it is frequently identified as *the* cause of child soldiering. This applies both in war situations
and in more peaceful circumstances where armies recruit young people.
In fact, the opposite clearly illustrates the point: the children of the rich
rarely do military service even when there is supposed to be universal
conscription.[12] A study of demobilized child soldiers in a transit center
in the Democratic Republic of Congo found that 61 percent of the three
hundred children surveyed said that their family had no income, and
more than half had at least six siblings.[13] This does not mean that
poverty in itself explains why children join armed conflict, but it is
obviously a strong contributory factor. Young people who are not living in impoverished circumstances are unlikely to join the armed forces
or armed groups, although there will always be exceptions.

The poverty may be a long-standing condition that is not, or is not
directly, related to the conflict:

> *My family is very poor, you see, actually, because, they haven't—
> sometimes she [mother] doesn't have enough to pay for schooling,
> going shopping, paying the rent, you see, a lot, you see, many things,
> how do I say it, there are many things she can't buy, sometimes she
> doesn't have any money.* ▪ Carlos, *Colombia*

Those who were already poor may be pulled even further down by the
conflict, or war may create or exacerbate a relative economic decline
of those who previously were not so badly off:

> *We faced terrible problems because of the war. If not for the war we
> would have lived happily. My family and most of the village suffered
> badly due to economical problems. At that time it was very difficult
> to earn money. We suffered a lot due to this.* ▪ Sabesan, *Sri Lanka*

*My mother was a nurse; my father was retired from the army. Before
the war, he had a bit of money, as he owned two buses and a mill for
fufu [cassava-based dough]. We lost everything through the war.*
■ Albert, *Congo-Brazzaville*

Poverty is a factor in its own right, but it also affects other critical
issues for young people such as the ability to access schooling, which in
turn limits the employment or other economic opportunities for young
people. All these aspects of general poverty tend to be exaggerated by war.

Education and Employment

The question of education (including vocational training) has a different
and more immediate impact on young people than on adults. Childhood
(in the broad sense) is the time of education—schooling, further education, or vocational training—and, in particular for adolescents, the
transition into gainful employment or other means of livelihood. In
addition to their socializing role, schools may have the opposite effect:
they may challenge dominant forms of socialization. Education has the
potential to bring about changes in values and attitudes. The scope of
possibility that schools offer may be cherished in societies that are open
to outside influences, or it may be spurned as the source of evil in societies that wish to insulate the population against these influences.
Schools that offer a modern education, including access to the natural
sciences and to technology, to social and historical analysis, and to an
international language, may be seen as liberating or as dangerous,
depending on the point of view.[14]

*I think our teachers were actually serving the government. In fact, we
looked upon them more as enemies than as friends.*
■ Samuel, *South Africa*[15]

For young people, access to education is a critical factor,[16] but the
content of the education and its relevance to employment, the way in
which they are treated in school, and whether the school itself operates
as a recruiting ground are also issues. In addition, not being in education or employment is a critical risk factor for young people. If they are
not involved in either education or employment, what are young people going to do to fill their time, to support themselves or their families,
and to give meaning to their lives?

The impact on the students, and the passion that it evoked, comes through clearly from the South African experience:

> *The SRC [Student Representative Council] was a body in school that was called upon whenever a rule was broken; they can go to the principal and say "this and this and this" is needed. On each and everything we need, the SRC has to stand for us. But the Boers and/or the police didn't want us to have SRC at school. But we fought for it, for the SRC. Some of the students died for the SRC.*
> ▪ Benny, *South Africa*

For some, lack of access to school is a long-standing problem not specifically related to the conflict, but often associated with poverty:

> *I didn't stop [school] voluntarily, it's because I didn't have any financial support. I was bright.* ▪ Henri, *Congo-Brazzaville*

> *I went to school only occasionally. Although school was free, I had hardly any books to write in and sometimes I did not have a pen.*
> ▪ Gajathukan, *Sri Lanka*

For others, it is the conflict that causes the closure of the schools, or they themselves are displaced by the conflict and thus the schools are no longer accessible to them.

Education shapes the understanding, attitudes, and behavior of individuals. Often military and political forces use the school curriculum as a tool for indoctrinating students to their cause.[17] Education can be used—deliberately or accidentally—to exacerbate and politicize the existing differences in a society so that these become the basis for, or help to perpetuate, violent conflict.[18] Three particular aspects deserve attention: the practice of segregated education, the quality of the education, and the use of schools as recruiting grounds.

In South Africa, segregated education existed as part of the segregation in other aspects of life. Although segregation is not government policy in Northern Ireland it is evident in reality in housing, sports, the media, and education. Over 90 percent of all schools are either Catholic or Protestant in ethos and practice. The reality of segregated education is that, in the main, Catholic and Protestant children do not meet each other. This emphasizes differences between them and encourages ignorance and suspicion:

Where does it trouble you to come into contact with Catholics?
[Long pause] What do you mean? Where do I?

When you're meeting them.
[Long pause] Like where would I meet them? [Long pause]
I haven't really met any. [Laughs] ▪ Paul, *Northern Ireland*

And what does that mean then if peace comes, what does that
mean [with respect] to your feelings about Catholics?
I still wouldn't mix with them; I know I'll never mix with
Catholics.

Do you know any?
[Laughs] No.

Have you ever met any?
No.

How do you know you haven't?
How do I know I haven't? Because I wouldn't associate myself
with them. ▪ David, *Northern Ireland*

For some, it is the quality of the education system itself that sets the
scene for their developing motivation to become involved. Elements of
the educational situation in South Africa were major factors in the political mobilization of youth, particularly in the townships. These included
the difficulty of access for those in poverty, the poor quality of the education that was available, corporal punishment, and then the Bantu Education Act introducing Afrikaans as the language of tuition. For many of
the young people it was the most immediate impact of the apartheid
system. This led them to become active through SRCs:

In South Africa, there was no good education since 1953. [. . .] As
a student, we were affected, because there was something called like
Afrikaans that was used in school. [. . .] in primary [. . .] we were not
aware about that. But as we went along we saw that it was wrong.
The Bantu Education was prioritizing Afrikaans and each subject was
going to be taught in Afrikaans. And then it was hated by each and
every student, because most students were against the Afrikaans.
Because we know one thing, that this is the kind of education that
was given at the same time we don't know the Afrikaans. The

Afrikaans is for the Boers. Understand? The quality of education was not good for us, understand?

So when did you start becoming aware that the education was not good for you and . . .
   I think I was doing Standard 5 in Cape Town . . .

Standard 5 . . .
   Yeah . . . .

What about your teachers? Did you have a good relationship with them? Did they tell you about the problems?
   No, at that time the teachers were aware of this, but . . . They did not want to lose their work, understand? So but there are some of the teachers who, whenever they were with us, they ask us and tell us everything about the kind of education we are in [whispers to emphasize the secretive nature of these discussions with their teachers], why this kind of education is frustrating . . . They just tell you about this . . . They gave us the real history, understand? So what I can say, some teachers were and others weren't . . . telling us everything and explaining to us what went wrong.

And how did the teachers think the education system could be changed? How did the teachers think the situation could change for your people?
   One thing . . . the People's Education, one education, one department, understand, of People's Education. Because what was happening in our school you found out . . . in the class there are so many students. Maybe there are sixty to eighty students in your class but there is one teacher. But if you go to white school [a school for whites only], you find that there are eighteen in the class, under-stand? So . . . at the same time . . . you found out there were no schools, there were few schools for the black boys, most of them . . . you find them learning under the trees, you understand? No schools were being built. You will find that they were learning in the church. They will cut the church [divide the church into "classrooms"], making rooms with the black plastic . . . Then . . . you found out that whenever there is a noise in the class, there is no good education that you can get [stumbling increases]. So at the same time, [for] those who were under the tree, if there is a rain, there is no school. So at the same time, at school there is corporal punishment.
                                                       ▪ Benny, *South Africa*

In some cases, the school or the teacher was a direct factor in motivating the students to join the armed struggle. In these and other ways, "schools are often battlegrounds for the hearts and minds of the next generation."[19]

In Pakistan, the *madrassahs* are private Islamic religious schools where tuition, room, and board are provided free, and the students are mostly from the poorest sectors:

Our schoolteacher used to tell us that Jihad [holy war against unbelievers] is a religious duty of every Muslim. ▪ Aziz, *Pakistan*

We were taught in the madrassah that one who sacrifices his life in Jihad, he is a martyr and will be rewarded generously. Besides he will recommend other people for Paradise in addition to rewarding him Paradise without judgment. ▪ Ehtesham, *Pakistan*

Once one of our teachers told us in a class that if we kill a Shiite Muslim we deserve to be a judge. He was a Pashtun. Whereas there was no sense of ethnic conflict between students, the Taliban was trying to create and stimulate those things. I am a Sunni. I never thought in my whole life about who religiously are my friends. I have never been sensitive to know if my classmates are Shiite or Sunni. ▪ Mustafa, *Afghanistan*

In the United Kingdom, educational institutions are used to promote recruitment to the armed forces through career days and displays. Sometimes, there is a close link between the school and the army. The Combined Cadet Forces[20] in the United Kingdom is based in 245 schools (194 independent and 51 in the state- or grant-maintained sector).[21] They receive assistance and support for their training program from the regular and reserve forces, but the bulk of adult support is provided by members of school staffs who are responsible to head teachers for the conduct of cadet activities.[22]

Often the school premises are used to make contact with the young people:

These regular soldiers come and talk to you. In my last year, I went on a school visit, to see an army stand. They spoke to all of us, like, gave us an initial brief because we were, like, school-leavers. There is, like, advertisement about what age you can join the army.
▪ Stephen, *United Kingdom*

Photo by M. Crozet

Schools are used to promote recruitment to the armed forces

This is not exclusive to the United Kingdom or to the regular armed forces:

> *The rebels came in the schools to speak to us and they said that we had to fight against Mobutu.* ▪ Vanessa, *DRC*

In other cases, the school is the place where action against a certain situation is being organized, and where young people come in contact with those people that are involved in the armed struggle, or are confronted with the reality of the conflict:

> *Specific things that made me join—I think indirectly the whole problem of being involved for myself started from basically the choice of selection of subjects and so on. It started there and then it spilled*

over. Because I think the SRC at that time were also timely in terms of telling us that "the reason why you cannot do what you want to do, because there is a government in power that does not want us to do all these things." ▪ Samuel, *South Africa*

I was a member of COSAS [Congress of South African Students] by then. What we were fighting for was a nonracial education. So COSAS was then the party who made the body of the Western Cape Student Congress and then with the Student Congress in other areas, in the Eastern Cape and others, we came together. So this body was going to politicize the students, was going to tell them that they have to be aware of the politics; we must be aware of what is happening in the country, what happened in our education, and how can we change this education to be the People's Education. [. . .] COSAS was there to advise the students what they can do to get the People's Education instead of the Bantu Education. So COSAS was politicizing us at school, at the same time there were workshops, and at the same time there was someone who was going to give us a paper, that is, something that tells us about the history of what happened, what happened in our country. Understand? So it was COSAS that inspired us [. . .] in joining the revolutionary army. ▪ Benny, *South Africa*

Ideally, education and vocational training should respond to demands in the labor market. Unfortunately this is often not the case and educated young people do not find appropriate jobs. This may be due to a general educational system that is not flexible enough to adapt to the changing labor market. In addition, armed conflict often has an impact on the economy by seriously reducing the already limited job opportunities. The relatively rapid changes in the economy trigger major changes in the demands for labor. All countries emerging from armed conflict face the challenge of adapting their education and vocational training systems to the new demands. For example, higher education in Congo-Brazzaville used to guarantee a job in the public sector. Now, many university graduates are unemployed. This leads to a general frustration, to a sense of personal failure and of letting down the family that has invested so many hopes for the future in the educational achievement of one of its members. These combine into a specific lack of motivation to pursue education:

Education does not lead to employment, so why bother? The State no longer recruits, you have a Ph.D. and you are a taxi man!
▪ Albert, *Congo-Brazzaville*

Similarly, during the apartheid years in South Africa, having a diploma did not change anything:

> *You can go to an industrial area and ask an employee: "What is your surname?" There is a lot of "Van. . . Van. . ." [typical surnames for Afrikaners or white people in South Africa]. They are all Afrikaans-speaking; they are all from the same house! They make it a family thing! Nothing of empowering people and all those things . . . And especially when you are black, you get the lowest position, regardless of your education.* ▪ Solomon, *South Africa*

For those who are making the transition from education to employment, there is a direct relationship between their school performance and the options open to them. Leaving school at an early age with low or no qualifications limits the choices available:

> *[In the army] you can go out and see the world. You can get life experience, OK. It proved that for me in my own personal point of view. It proved that if you've got no qualifications, no GCSEs [General Certificate of Secondary Education] or if you've got them and they're poor, it proves you don't have to go and work in a factory. Doing the same thing day in, day out. Bored, you know.*
> ▪ Stephen, *United Kingdom*

For others, unemployment seems inevitable because of the war or the general economic situation in the country.[23] Where there appears to be only one alternative route available, it is not surprising that this is the one these adolescents take:

> *The shortest route, the easiest job in Congo is the army: they are always hiring; above all they are paid.* ▪ Albert, *Congo-Brazzaville*

> *Everyone wants to go in the army because there's no more work, there's no more factory. That's why the young people want to wear the military outfit.* ▪ Pascal, *Congo-Brazzaville*

> *We, all the youngsters, thought it was natural to join the LTTE [Liberation Tigers of Tamil Eelam] since there were no standard jobs on offer; my brothers have done the same, and so have most others.*
> ▪ Sudhahar, *Sri Lanka*

> *No, I'm on the brew [unemployed, receiving state social security benefits].* ▪ Paul, *Northern Ireland*

The linkage between education and employment works in several different ways. Education that is considered unlikely to lead to employment is seen as pointless and irrelevant by many adolescents, and so they are more likely to drop out or to behave in ways that lead to their exclusion from school. Those who are in education are not seeking employment. If young people are neither in education nor employed, the need to find some other form of activity is great, either to ensure a means of economic survival for themselves and possibly their families, and/or to avoid boredom. Thus employment may be seen as having a social as well as an economic function:

The main cause of going there was unemployment, I think. I had nothing to do here so I went there. If you have some business or you are studying then you do not think about taking part in Jihad.
> ▪ Aziz, *Pakistan*

Family and Friends

The direct family, the extended family, community, friends, and sometimes other people such as sports coaches or teachers together form the social support network that is one of the most important influences on young people and the choices they make.

Of these, the family situation is the most significant factor in the involvement or noninvolvement of young people in armed forces or armed groups. Although family, or the lack of it, obviously also affects adults, it is in the nature of childhood that the family environment has a proportionally greater impact for good or ill and is perhaps the single greatest influence for all adolescents. In "normal" life, the family is recognized as being a major factor in the development of children and in their choice of profession or occupation; what is extraordinary is how little attention has been given to it as a factor in involvement in warfare. This may reflect the relative lack of attention that has been paid specifically to adolescents and their reasons for becoming involved in armed conflict. Although the family's presence, absence, or role comes through as a major factor in the general environmental context of these young people, its importance increases as the critical moment of decision is approached.

For some, involvement in the military is a normal and acceptable part of family life. When parents, siblings, or other family members are involved with the military, joining up seems natural, particularly if this is combined with a religious, ethnic, or ideological element to the family involvement[24]:

> *I come from a warrior's family; as far as I remember, my father has always been in the rebellion.* ▪ Catherine, DRC

> *The main reason for my involvement was the family environment, as all of our elders fought in Afghanistan. I was socialized in such an environment, so my joining was somehow very normal, I say. Joining was not a problem at all because my father was a commander himself.* ▪ Khalid, *Pakistan*

> *I was two years old when my father died. . . . I have two elder brothers; the first one joined LTTE and he died a hero's death in battle. The second one also joined LTTE.* ▪ Sudhahar, *Sri Lanka*

> *[My father] was a military officer.* ▪ Mustafa, *Afghanistan*

> *My da [father] was in the army.* ▪ Billy, *Northern Ireland*

> *I had brothers in the paramilitaries . . . and about seven uncles.*
> ▪ Jessica, *Colombia*

For others, the family might not be directly involved in military action, but was in the movement or supported the political ends:

> *My parents did not approve of what I did, but my grandmother did—she was a member of the PAC [Pan-African Congress]. My grandmother would tell me about the activities of the PAC. [. . .] she would also provide a place to sleep for those who needed it.*
> ▪ Solomon, *South Africa*

> *My father, he is a person who always supported the [Black] Consciousness Movement, even during the days of the struggle. He was always vocal about these things, and then, unconsciously, you also pick it up. And my father, he also had some bad encounters with the apartheid system. It rubbed off on us as well.*
> ▪ Samuel, *South Africa*

The family environment that predisposes to involvement in armed conflict may be the lack of family—acting as a push rather than a pull factor. Children without family or who are separated from their family are recognized as being especially vulnerable to both forced and voluntary recruitment[25]:

> *My father left when I was a child, then my mother got married with another man.* ▪ Vanessa, DRC

> *Almost all my family disappeared, to start with my dad, who passed away. We were so poor, and because of the wars, the worries, our dad died, our mom too; the members of our family were dispersed in the bush.* ▪ Urbain, DRC

> *My family is not there anymore [. . .] they died during the conflict, they are all dead . . . The soldiers came in the villages, they plundered and killed everybody, they raped the women, the girls; they killed everyone, even the children.* ▪ Christine, DRC

For others, repeated flight was an important issue, aligned with the more general disruption of family and family life:

> *When I was one year old I came to Iran with my mother, but when my father was killed in 1983 we returned to Afghanistan. So it was the second time. We migrated to Iran because the Taliban was bothering and beating us.* ▪ Ali, Afghanistan

It is notable that Germain (DRC) was considered an exceptional case—"nobody can understand how he could have been enrolled; even within the [Demobilization] Centre, they are all surprised" (DRC interviewer)—because he joined up when he was living with both parents and not in poverty. It may be relevant that Germain's parents were often absent from home for their work.

The peer group is another major influence on adolescents. This is equally true in relation to their perceived identity in general and the particular pressure to join an armed group. As with the other environmental factors identified, this does not mean that all the young people in a group will join but that where many of the members of a group are already involved or are considering joining, the pressure to join is greater:

> *Aye, aye, most of the people that I run about with are in it. All my mates, or 100 percent of my mates are in it, or 99 percent, because there's other mates I have and they're not even in it, but you don't really say much to them ones. 'Cause most of my mates are in it and*

Photo by A.P. Marti

Friends from childhood often join the same outfit together

that's the way I've grown up. Even the commanders of the UDA [Ulster Defence Army], like, they're like your mates, they go out with you and buy you drinks and they're in your band. So if you go out with them you're talking away with them, you're mates with them, then you just get on like good mates. ▪ Billy, *Northern Ireland*

Most of my friends are in it, so they are. Went in through it that way, like. But I'm in a flute band too, it's a UDA flute band, and I was in it before I was in it and then just joined it, you know.
▪ Paul, *Northern Ireland*

The young people who are already in the "company," they encourage you. ▪ Pierre, *Congo-Brazzaville*

All my friends from my childhood, the ones I used to play cars with, play bandits, they're all in the same outfit now . . . the people who like this get a taste for it. ▪ Carlos, *Colombia*

There was a group of students, we were about 16—and we came together and had a meeting from time to time. And, hmm, finally he set up the meeting to go into exile, the procedure. And that is basically how it went. We got passports, we were taken from here, and from [a nearby town] we were taken by car. ▪ Samuel, *South Africa*

Politics and Ideology

The political context in which young people grow up is of course relevant in influencing their perception. Being part of a family and peer group that opposes the authorities creates an identity different from those who are part of the ruling class. Without examining the political situation of the countries concerned, it is clear that this sets the general context and influences the individual's specific environment. As a result, some young people join out of conviction with strong ideological motivation.

For some there is the sense of the need to overturn an oppressive regime. The young people may also see, and personally suffer from, acts that they perceive as symptomatic of this regime:

Mobutu and his soldiers, they were mean, they oppressed us, tormented us, we were always mistreated. [. . .] He and his men! Once they had beaten me because of my boots! Till this day, I have hated them. When I was small, I had fashionable clothes, and I had boots like military boots; it was fashionable in Congo. But not everyone could have some because they were expensive. Once my mother bought me some. Once I left for school with my boots, I was proud. A soldier called me over and said to me to come to him, and he asked me, "Who gave you a soldier's boots?" [. . .] The soldier told me to remove them [. . .] I told them that it was my mom who had bought these for me. They didn't care. The guy started to strike my back with a cord that hurts. I bled. ▪ Germain, DRC

I joined the AFDL [Alliance des Forces Démocratiques pour la Liberation du Congo-Zaire] to drive out Mobutu, to drive out misery, to make the life better. . . . I'm waiting for the Good Samaritan who will come to help me. I am tired: too much demagogy, too many promises, and at the end, nothing. ▪ Michel, DRC

I was so young, you see. They [the commanders] wanted me to go to school, to continue my education. [. . .] I wanted to go back to South Africa to fight for the freedom of the country. We were the young generation—our time had come. ▪ Solomon, South Africa

It is more that you have to—what you want to change, you have to make and bring some changes—towards a just society. That is the main reason. ▪ Kathryn, South Africa

When the Russians occupied Afghanistan, my father began to fight with them. Before the war my father's job was not to fight but he

*taught military training. When the war started he began to fight.
We all fought for the freedom of our homeland. . . . In 1999 I entered
the war. . . . Before that time I was a cultural soldier. I did propaganda for supporting the warriors . . . to free the country from the
control of foreigners.* ▪ Mustafa, *Afghanistan*

*If I wanted to live under the Taliban there was no enjoyment in
our life because the Taliban regime was following a racist policy.
We had no choice except fighting [against] the Taliban. There was
hope that if I fight the Taliban and if I kick them out there would
be a better life for the rest of my family, even if I were killed.*
▪ Ali, *Afghanistan*

*I joined after having seen the sufferings of the population; I decided
to drive out Mobutu's men, who maltreated us. There were great
difficulties, especially to study, too much annoyance.* ▪ Joseph, *DRC*

Often current wars are labelled as ethnic or religious conflicts in
countries where the ethnic groups used to live side-by-side and different
religions were practised in one village or even family. Political leaders
sometimes use the differences between people and exaggerate them to
create fear in order to mobilize recruits to join in the fighting. Some
political leaders and warlords have been successful in transmitting these
differentiating messages, thus contributing to the voluntary participation
of large numbers of young people. In such situations, religion and ethnicity are not so much the causes of youth participation in armed conflict but rather contributing factors that are part of the political context
in which they grow up:

*Because I wanted to be fighting for the cause of the Protestant people.
I didn't like the way Sinn Fein/IRA [Irish Republican Army] ran
about and shot innocent Protestant people, and blew up Protestant
people, decent Protestant people. [. . .] The Ulster Young Militants is
a group set up to defend the people of this estate from the Catholics
trying to break into our houses, who want to come in and fire shots,
to come in and shoot people, come in and blow the place up.*
▪ David, *Northern Ireland*

*It is obligatory on every Muslim to fight nonbelievers. Moreover,
the religious class [clergy, etc.] propagates the philosophy of Jihad
as a shortcut to win the grace of Allah. The ultimate outcome is
martyrdom for which he [the martyr] will be awarded Paradise.*
▪ Khalid, *Pakistan*

I fought for the sake of my belief and for Islam. . . . It was our Islamic duty to fight against infidelity. It was also a national duty upon us to fight against foreigners and occupiers. ▪ Ali, *Afghanistan*

What made me hold the weapon? It's that the Mbochis [ethnic group from Northern Congo] were ungrateful. They started to threaten us; we, the Tcheks. Me, I could not tolerate it, to let my people suffer. I am Tchek, I would remain Tchek. ▪ Pascal, *Congo-Brazzaville*

Specific Features of Adolescence

Any analysis of the factors that lead young people into joining armed forces or armed groups cannot be complete if their adolescence, as a significant moment in their personal development, is not itself taken into account. Indeed, it can provide an additional explanation for much of their behavior, choices, and the way they internalize the events happening around them. Although the term "adolescent" may not be used in all cultures, there is wide recognition that there is a period when the young person is no longer a "child" but not yet an "adult," although increasingly expected or required to take on some adult roles and activities. It can be a difficult time for both the young person and the family as well as other adults who have to deal with them. They may seem like adults, able to take care of themselves. They may be perpetrators of physical and sexual violence as well as its victims. They may challenge authority and rebel against restrictions, while at the same time they need support, encouragement, and moral and emotional guidance.

According to the developmental theory of Erik Erikson,[26] adolescence is a period during which the self-image of a young person is very important. At the same time, the individual is constantly focusing on the reaction of "significant others," such as friends and family members, and will try to adopt behavior and/or appearance that conform to the ideal style of the moment. The impact of such influences inside armed groups or at the time of signing up should not be underestimated:

There were two of my cousins who had joined the LTTE. They used to come home in the night carrying arms. I really did not understand the meaning behind this big war when I was small, but I used to be attracted by the uniforms and the guns, even though I could only touch the guns. They used to boast of their heroic experience.
▪ Sathiyan, *Sri Lanka*

In a context of personal determination, the adolescent can be encouraged to search for identity in a destructive or negative way, by being cruel and intolerant with people that are considered different (for example, because of their skin color, culture, or clothes). This makes young people easily influenced by propaganda that can reinforce their existing intolerance and incite them to take up arms against people that are designated as enemies:

> *Because I personally believe that when people are young, others can abuse them. It is my very unfortunate fate that I was drawn into wars.* ▪ Javad, *Afghanistan*

Adolescence also generates feelings of strength and power, a direct result of the physical and intellectual maturity the young person feels:

> *It was actually really nice to be able to do something on my own. At the time I was, how do you say, starting to feel more confident, more free to do what I wanted really. It was nice. It was nice to be able to go out somewhere, to find out and do what I want.*
> ▪ Andrew, *United Kingdom*

> *I believed that I was an adult, and I had nothing else. I said to myself that it would be good for me, and then the young people who are already in the "company," they encourage you.*
> ▪ Pierre, *Congo-Brazzaville*

There are a number of features that could make an armed group attractive in adolescents' eyes, but it is the impression of invulnerability—that all difficulties can be overcome—that influences the decision whether or not to join. The real dangers connected to being a soldier tend to be overlooked or ignored:

> *It was my friends that encouraged me to become a Cobra. They told me that it was not dangerous. I could hold the weapon, they said. Above all, there was a good ambience, it's not complicated. When they return with money; you want to have some too!*
> ▪ Albert, *Congo-Brazzaville*

> *I was not thinking of fighting. I just wanted to enjoy and have a nice trip.* ▪ Ajith, *Sri Lanka*

> *I joined the FARC [Revolutionary Armed Forces of Colombia] because, well, because I was lonely, because I was fed up with my*

*mom, because I didn't think that that was [. . .] going to change my
life, I thought that I was standing on top of the world.*
▪ Carolina, *Colombia*

This is compounded by the tendency in adolescence to be rather opportunistic, taking immediate benefits seriously:

*You see people fighting, earning money, then you want to make the
same.* ▪ Pierre, *Congo-Brazzaville*

The context of war might also provide the young people with
opportunities. They can become important members of their families in
terms of protection or helping them survive by providing them with an
income or food. This may be seen by them as an individual opportunity,
or it may be a responsibility thrust upon them by becoming the head of
the family, by being expected to provide economically for the family or
to give protection—particularly in the case of boys:

*I thought that what I did was normal, because it was to save my
family. . . . all that I did, it was because I wanted my family to
survive.* ▪ Henri, *Congo-Brazzaville*

This perceived societal role may be extended beyond the family to the
community more generally,[27] providing an opportunity to become important members, especially through the defense forces:

*I began hearing about the Indigenous Guards about a year ago, when
I was told that in the Guards you were given a stick to guard with,
you had to be aware of who was coming in or going out, and it was
a post that required a lot of responsibility. . . . For me, it's a process,
an organization of young people, who look after the lives of the other
members of their community.* ▪ Otoniel, *Colombia*

Traditional beliefs and community perceptions about the entry of
boys into manhood also play a specific part. Male adolescents are often
expected to protect and provide for their family and community, including taking up arms,[28] while this is not the expected role of girls:

Just protecting your area. Simple as that. ▪ David, *Northern Ireland*

*We are working as SDUs, Self-Defence Units. . . . For example,
whenever they came to the area, maybe the vigilantes come and burn*

the houses. So we have to guard the area. ▪ Benny, *South Africa*

The UDA, that's what stops the hooding [petty crime] 'round here. If there was no UDA there'd be like houses getting broke into, people's cars, you know, every minute of the day, just robberies, and people getting hassled and things happening. But it's the UDA stops it all, it's them that keeps policing the areas. ▪ Paul, *Northern Ireland*

Others use this situation as a way of escaping from their parents' guardianship. Under those circumstances, joining an armed group can in fact offer the possibility to survive outside the family:

I just got fed up with being at home, I don't know if it was because of how my family treated me, or my mom, or my dad, or whether it was because I was ungrateful to them, I don't know if it's because of that, that I was fed up, but yes, I got on well with them for a while, then it got a bit bitter, but anyway, I decided to leave home. I left home when I was ten years old. ▪ Alfredo, *Colombia*

Culture and Tradition

Culture and tradition provide the individual with a framework through which to observe and interpret what is happening, influencing the way they see and interpret things. The place of the individual in society, determined by their family and clan, their age, sex, and religion, and the profession of their parents, is an important concept to take into account when trying to understand motivations of young people to become combatants. The whole set of rules and regulations surrounding their culturally determined role in society is very different from one context to another. The tradition of warfare, with its rules on the way war should be fought, includes ideas on who should be fighting and who should not:

Afghanistan's situation was so that all people from 15 years old to 80 had to fight. ▪ Mortaza, *Afghanistan*

They like me because I joined the local regiment and everything. They always like to keep it in the family and everything, so that's why I suppose they keep an interest. Even though they don't even know me, they're very supportive of me. ▪ Stephen, *United Kingdom*

It also provides guidance on the accepted levels of violence allowed. Although cultures and traditions are not static, adapting to new challenges, the norms and values carried through them are important elements that contribute to the decision to join or not.

In Afghanistan, family involvement in armed conflict has become a cultural tradition for some:

All Afghani families have always had guns. From a long time before the recent wars, Afghans carried guns with themselves. Because Afghanistan has never been secure, people had to be armed to keep and defend themselves. • Mortaza, *Afghanistan*

My father was a Mojahed and he himself led a group of Mojahedin. In the early years, my father led a group . . . and later my brother led it. • Hassan, *Afghanistan*

In Colombia the culture of violence and arms is so prevalent that some see it as unnatural not to have or like weapons:

Because all my life I've liked guns . . . Because I was brought up by my family and they also like guns. • Jessica, *Colombia*

We used to live with an aunt, and my cousin was one of the lads from there, he was one of the tough ones, and so I used to see all these things going on there. He had his finger in a bit of everything. I mean, we lived on a corner, and they used to sit there and practice shooting and so I used to watch them and I learned . . . I got used to that, and so . . • Andrés, *Colombia*

The media (in particular radio and television) both reflect and help to create or perpetuate the cultural values, as well as often being the source of information (and interpretation) about the conflict:

Even at a young age, you see it on the TV. Even when you go to primary school you get books that say, "This is a policeman, this is a fireman, this is a soldier." [. . .] from a young age, you're aware of the army. It is a national thing. [. . .] Everyone knows about the army and everyone learns about it. • Stephen, *United Kingdom*

By listening to the radio, from gangs from the same group, you see, they were beginning to get together. Law enforcement was here all the time, gangs were broken up, many gangs, many armed

Artwork created by former young soldiers portrays scenes of war

people, you see, bad people, like those people from the "pit" over there. ▪ Carlos, *Colombia*

When I was working at the poultry farm I heard on radio as well as television that a fierce war broke out at Parwun.

▪ Muhammad, *Pakistan*

Sometimes, radio and television are used as direct tools for recruitment:

The rebels called to the people on the radio, many young people joined at this time. ▪ Vanessa, *DRC*

Others are influenced by movies and movie characters:

One day, we will loot over there; on that I am categorical. This day there, I would make at least 15 VX [large cars] over there. I will plant my name over there. It will be over with Pascal, I would be General Braddock.

Braddock, is that a film character?
It's Chuck Norris . . . [Pascal]

Oh yeah, it's Chuck Norris in Missing in Action.[29]
Pascal dreams he's playing war games. [Albert]
▪ Pascal and Albert, *Congo-Brazzaville*

It was a matter of influence; you look at action films; when you look at that you are impressed! I said to myself, "Why just him?" I said to myself that one day, it would be me; I could also do that. Learning how to use a gun, fighting in the front line, knowing how it happens.

What kind of action film did you watch?
Commando, Rambo! [Laughter]

OK, but for example Commando it's an extreme case, but Rambo at the end, it's fast and furious!
He dies, but there's all that action!

Yes, he kills a lot of people!
Yes, OK, but I didn't think of killing people; I thought more about the fighting and shooting.

Yes, but when he shoots, he kills people.
Yes . . . [Laughter] You see, at the beginning I didn't think of that, because I watched the television, and I didn't know about the

consequences and how it could happen, and so on. I didn't think of that, I was still a kid. I was so impressed by the action, the way they handled weapons , the way they dressed. I said to myself that one day, I would wear the same outfit. ▪ Germain, DRC

Conclusion

War itself is the most crucial and fundamental environmental factor in the participation of young people in warfare. As long as wars continue, young people will become involved. This does not mean that nothing can be done without abolishing war completely.

The causal effects of war are not only direct, but also indirect. The impact of armed conflict extends to families, the economy, the education system, and employment or other means of economic livelihood for young people themselves and for their parents, and creates a need for self-protection and protection of other members of the family. Each of these elements can play a role in a young person's decision to take up arms. In societies where the military (whether government or armed group) provides status and role models as well as the means of livelihood, and for whom identity (religious, ethnic, peer group) is bound up in the understanding of the conflict, there need to be strong counter-factors if young people are not to become involved.

While the presence of war itself is important, this does not explain why some young people in war zones join and others do not (nor, of course, why young people join armed forces in peacetime). Clearly the specific combination of the different environmental factors makes some significantly more vulnerable. However, the factors are also cumulative; thus a poor child, living in a war zone, without family, education, or employment, is seriously at risk of becoming involved.

In addition to war, what begins to emerge here is that an individual's family and education are critical factors: they may directly or indirectly (through presence, absence, and attitude) make the difference, for the at-risk young person, between joining and not doing so.

Notes

1. This is supported by Dumas and de Cock (2003), where the situation of child recruits and a control group are compared (p. 25).

2. For general background information, see Appendix 2: Sri Lanka conflict profile.

3. For general background information, see Appendix 2: Northern Ireland conflict profile. To distinguish between the two groups of young people from the United Kingdom, we refer to Northern Ireland and the United Kingdom separately (the United Kingdom is made up of England, Scotland, Wales, and Northern Ireland). All interviewees from Northern Ireland are associated with Loyalist paramilitary groups. Regrettably, despite the best efforts of the research team concerned, it did not prove possible to obtain interviews with those young people associated with Republican paramilitary groups because of the sensitive situation in relation to the cease-fire.

4. For general background information, see Appendix 2: Colombia conflict profile.

5. Brett and McCallin (1998) identified changing sides as one of the distinctive features of *child* (as opposed to adult) soldiering, in situations where the child's involvement is opportunistic, because of their normalization into violence or lack of choice. Changes may be because of the ebb and flow of the balance of advantage, or because of capture and incorporation into the capturing armed forces or group. This aspect of child soldiering was also commented on in relation to Central Africa by Dumas and de Cock (2003, p. 19).

6. For general background information, see Appendix 2: Congo conflict profile.

7. For general background information, see Appendix 2: Sierra Leone conflict profile.

8. The use of the term "recreation" is interesting because it makes the link with the concept of "recreational rioting" referred to in the Northern Ireland case study.

9. Those interviewed in Pakistan speak of their experience as volunteers in Afghanistan.

10. For general background information, see Appendix 2: Democratic Republic of Congo conflict profile.

11. If poverty is defined as living on less than $1 per day, the number of youth (15–24-year-olds) living in poverty is about 238 million; and if the broader definition of $2 is used, the number rises to 462 million. *World Youth Report 2003*.

12. Brett and McCallin 1998.

13. Crill 2000.

14. Chung 1999, p. 1.

15. For general background information, see Appendix 2: South Africa conflict profile.

16. Richards (1996) explores the question of whether denial of education was a factor in the actual war in Sierra Leone, which he describes as a drama of social exclusion, and not only a factor in certain adolescents getting involved in it.

17. Sommers 2002.

18. Bush and Saltarelli 2000, p. 9.

19. Chung 1999, p. 1.

20. The Cadet Forces in the United Kingdom include four groups: the Sea Cadet Corps, the Army Cadet Forces, the Air Training Corps, and the Combined Cadet Forces.

21. www.mod.uk/aboutus/factfiles/cadets.htm (consulted 5 May 2003).

22. www.rfca.org.uk/tav_rmc.htm (consulted 5 May 2003).

23. According to the *World Youth Report 2003,* youth (15–24 years old) make up more than 40 percent of the world's total unemployed, and "increasingly, the distinction between employment and unemployment has lost much of its meaning, as young people move in and out of informal activities where neither term has any real relevance"(p. 4).

24. McConnan and Uppard 2001, p. 40.

25. Brett and McCallin 1998; McConnan and Uppard 2001, p. 54.

26. Erikson 1972.

27. McConnan and Uppard, 2001, p. 53.

28. Ibid., p. 39.

29. A Vietnam war film.

2

The Life of the Prospective Volunteer

The environmental conditions identified in the previous chapter set the context without which young people rarely become involved in armed conflict. However, in no situation in which many or even all of these environmental factors exist, do all children become involved in the conflict. This chapter explores the reasons why some young people are more likely to join the armed forces or armed groups than others in the same general situation. Similar broad categories can be used to cluster their reasons: war and insecurity, economic motivation, education, family and friends, politics, and identity and psychosocial factors.

It is important to reiterate first that this study treats only those who were not abducted or physically forced but had some apparent measure of choice about joining, and second, that the focus is on the adolescent age group, rather than younger children, and that the perspective is that of the young people themselves.

War and Insecurity

As noted in the previous chapter, war is itself a cause of many of the other factors affecting the likelihood of involvement in the conflict, but war creates particular problems and dynamics over and above these. Living in the middle of a war or war-related context creates insecurity at several levels: physical, economic, and social. A sense of vulnerability is an important contributory factor in the decision. However, the degree of importance to particular individuals depends on their specific situation.

Adolescents face many different protection needs. These may be the general problems of personal physical protection related to the nature of the conflict:

You have no choice, to defend yourself, to be safe, you have to be armed. ▪ François, *Congo-Brazzaville*

When it's the war and you are a woman, you risk your life; you risk your life because you are a woman and the men will rape you if you don't protect yourself. ▪ Christine, *DRC*

For some, it is protection from recruitment or harassment by the other side, in particular as they approach "military age."[1]

The risk of being taken by the army was bigger as we grew older, and when we joined the LTTE, we had guns to protect ourselves and other Tigers to protect us. ▪ Sudhahar, *Sri Lanka*

While we were struggling to earn a little money to exist, the Sri Lankan army started giving us a lot of trouble. I was often caught and forced to work for them in their camps or outside clearing the areas or cutting bunkers. When I was caught like this till evening I worked for them without money, then I cannot earn anything for my family. I hated working for them. What I hated most was that every Sunday I had to go to their camp and sign in like a released prisoner. After all, what wrong have I done? Only thing was we were Tamil and young. Many of the men and young boys like me had to go to sign and all of us were given different assignments to complete. We came home tired, hungry, and angry. We felt helpless because there was no one to turn to for justice and relief. [. . .] I had to be free, so I decided to join the LTTE who were fighting against this type of situation. ▪ Sathiyan, *Sri Lanka*

First of all, I decided to join the paramilitaries because I was alone, and then with so many people having scores to settle with you, you need a bit of help. If someone's going to attack you, they can defend you. If I wouldn't have joined, I'd be dead. If you leave them, you are without protection. ▪ Andrés, *Colombia*

They're the ones that like help you when you're stuck, and if there's people bullying you, and all that, like you get round here all the time. And you get, like, people in different paramilitaries trying to bully you into giving them money, saying you owe me money and all this. ▪ Billy, *Northern Ireland*

But also, once you are in trouble, joining an armed group may be the only apparent way forward:

Because, well, I started looking around, and I thought if I've got no one watching my back then I'm going to get killed, because someone had a score to settle with me there in Toledo, everywhere, I was . . . In Toledo, well, the, the people that killed my cousins were looking for me and, and my brother and another cousin, I mean their other brother, to kill us. [. . .] I did it as a kind of refuge. . . . For that reason, on the one hand because of that situation, a lot of it was to do with the disregard people showed me. I said to myself, "This is great, I can have friends that appreciate me, that don't humiliate me." And here I found that, and I like it and I stayed here. ▪ Richard, *Colombia*

For some, joining seemed completely natural because of the apparent lack of other options:

I didn't choose this situation. You know that we are in a country at war, and then you don't have much choice. You can run away or fight. ▪ Christine, *DRC*

What else can I do? There's nothing else for me to do. I needed something to do so I decided to join. ▪ David, *Northern Ireland*

Economic Motivation

Only rarely are soldiers without food. Long after the civilian population is destitute and starving, armed soldiers are able to live reasonably well. For many young people this is the bottom line. If they or their families are not to go hungry, or even starve to death, becoming one of the soldiers seems the only or best option:

When the AFRC came to Koidu town after they had been driven from Freetown, they found us in Koidu and there was no way of leaving the town. We also did not have any food and water. We were starving. One could only get food then when one was with the rebels. That was what led me to live with them. ▪ Arthur, *Sierra Leone*

> *I was in my village when they attacked then. We all ran out of the town. Then I was given information that the RUF [Revolutionary United Front] had a lot of food. So we were with all members of my family, we had no rice, so I decided to go to the town and I lived with them.* ▪ Elisabeth, *Sierra Leone*

For others, it may not be as stark as starvation, but involvement may be a means of covering the basic necessities:

> *They've helped me get work before. You know, window cleaning. Say you've no money—when I first moved into the house, they bought me stuff for it and all, so they did. [. . .] Gave me tables, units, just stuff to help me out, like, when I first moved in because I wasn't [working] or nothing. Well, I was working but then I got sacked. So once I was on the thing [receiving unemployment benefit], like, they helped me out.* ▪ Paul, *Northern Ireland*

Adolescents are particularly likely to succumb to promises of pay or rewards because of their low economic status as young people, in

Photo by M. Crozet

Many join because there are no other options

addition to the fact that most of them come from families that are already poor or have been impoverished because of the war. Sometimes these promises are fulfilled, sometimes not:

> *As you know, there was no work here, so joining up paid [. . .] Above all, in this case you were allowed to loot, so you went in the banks, the safes, the taxis.* ▪ Albert, *Congo-Brazzaville*

> *It's a guaranteed wage.* ▪ Andrew, *United Kingdom*

> What was the main reason you asked to go to Northern Ireland?
> *Because I heard you'd get more money, ya'know. Because I was young and I wasn't on much compared to . . . I'd just turned 17. The army works its pay band like the younger you are the less money you get, even though you're doing exactly the same job.*
> ▪ Stephen, *United Kingdom*[2]

> *I was there when some guerrillas came by, and so I went and talked to them, and I wanted to join them, and so they [said] that if I wanted to join them then, they said that it was a good life with them. They told me that they got money, they got given clothes, and well, sometimes you had to go hungry, but there was money there— then when I got there, I found that that was just lies, being paid.*
> ▪ Alfredo, *Colombia*

Often, armies and armed groups also make promises of rewards to come after the conflict. Some promises are particularly attractive to young people as it gives them hope of a better future:[3]

> *They promised that we would build schools; they had promised the final count for the work done to defend our nation. [. . .] They owe us money, somewhere between $3,000 and $5,000 each. [. . .] When we enrolled they made a promise to us, and now that they have what they wanted, they must give us what they had promised to us.*
> ▪ Germain, *DRC*

> *I had decided to join to win the will of Almighty Allah because Allah has promised the reward of Paradise for martyrs of Jihad.*
> ▪ Ehtesham, *Pakistan*

The economic aspect is not purely individual selfishness. For some, the motivation is to benefit their families:

At that moment, I didn't think of my age. I felt like a brave man.
After having heard the promises of Kabila, I immediately thought of
my family, I said to myself that my family would be fine, that the
Mobutu men would be driven out; I didn't think of my age, I just
said to myself that I had to be in the army. I said to myself that if
I arrived at Kinshasa, I would have what I wanted. ▪ Joseph, DRC

We also got benefits on food rations and LTTE taxes because my
brother died a hero. ▪ Sudhahar, *Sri Lanka*

Because of the looting [. . .] You see them returning with a lot of
merchandise, and I had to take care of my family.
▪ Albert, *Congo-Brazzaville*

Most of the young people took up arms because it was too hard to
resist. Life was too hard. Most of us took up arms to get their families
out of misery. Me, I took up arms because we couldn't live any more,
most of the villages were destroyed, we had nothing; I had to help my
family. ▪ Henri, *Congo-Brazzaville*

Education

Because this research focuses specifically on adolescents, school (or the
lack of it) is a significant issue. Next to war and the role of the family,
this emerges as the major factor that influences the decision to join
armed forces or armed groups.

The fact of not being physically present in school greatly increases
a young person's vulnerability to recruitment because it leaves them
looking for other things to do. This absence from school can have different causes. Sometimes, lack of means prevents young people from
attending school:

I, I got to, I got to fourth grade and then my mom didn't have any
more money and I had to leave. ▪ Carlos, *Colombia*

I studied up to the ninth grade. The family had financial difficulties
and then I had to start working to help my family.
▪ Gajathukan, *Sri Lanka*

As we went through a lot of financial difficulties, I gave up my
studies and started working with my father. I had to work to support
my father who could not manage to support our family all by himself.
▪ Sathiyan, *Sri Lanka*

I continued my schooling in a school called Martyr Khatibi. I never was successful in school because when I was in my uncle's home I didn't have mental and social security in home and my uncle's wife tortured me. I didn't score good points in school. When I came to the seminary home I had to work for getting money. ▪ Javad, *Afghanistan*

Although this could be seen as, and indeed is, part of the more general issue of poverty, its specific impact in relation to the actual (as opposed to theoretical) availability of school is what affects the young people in this instance.

Other young people are excluded from school because of their behavior. Often this reflects other factors that already indicate vulnerability to recruitment:

At thirteen, I got threw out [of school]. [. . .] Smoking weed [. . .] That's what it was, I got caught and threw out for it. [. . .] I needed something to do so I decided to join.
▪ David, *Northern Ireland*

I was well behaved, then I started getting involved in the gang, and that's where it started going wrong for me, because I used to go to school and everything, until I was thrown out of school. . . . Yes, that's why I was expelled, I had some problems with my schoolmates. . . . I started there, I was new, you see, and you know that at school sometimes, sometimes there are gangs and so I was given a lot of hassle. . . . Because I was very quiet, you see, they saw that I was quiet, and so they started saying things to me, and then in the end I started insulting them, and then once I was going to kill a companion of mine, and so that's why I was expelled and that's when the problems started. ▪ Andrés, *Colombia*

One day when someone was going to kill me [. . .] I was 11 years old. I was at school, at school, some enemies of mine were studying there, and then in the end I was expelled because I fired a few shots off there, I shot at someone but he ran away. ▪ Carlos, *Colombia*

People were always trying to get us into trouble in the classroom, and we, we, we were so young, but we weren't going to let them get to us like that, and so the two of us went and got a knife, we bought it together, the two of us with our lunch money that we'd been given. So we were there with the knife and the kids looking at us, and so we took out the knife, and then we went like this towards the desk, and at

*once the teacher seeing the knife took it off us, and so—and that
happened, and we'd just bought it, we had it, and I don't know, so we
just started hitting her with a stick, but the head teacher, he was like,
"No, this family is a disgrace to this school," and we were expelled,
and so I didn't go back to that school.* ▪ Richard, *Colombia*

Some were not excluded by the school but simply dropped out:

*Actually, at the beginning, I was at school and that didn't work.
Me, I didn't like to go to school. Then I was lazing around in the
neighborhood, and then people come to see you. They ask you what
you want to do, and you see people fighting, earning money, then you
want to make the same.* ▪ Pierre, *Congo-Brazzaville*

*Even if I went to school I do not think I will benefit because I
will someday only be a fisherman like my father.*
▪ Shutharsan, *Sri Lanka*

*I was studying at school but I was not interested in education and
repeatedly dropped out from school on an annual basis, and instead
loved to fight [Jihad] as it was more attractive than education. I love
the spirit of fighting Jihad.* ▪ Zahid, *Pakistan*

Or again their lack of interest led to antisocial behavior at school, which
in turn led to their exclusion:

*Because of my school background. When I went to secondary school,
from the age of 12, I would have made my mind up to join the army.
I did read somewhere I needed no formal qualifications. And I didn't
really like school. [. . .] The way I saw school is that I wasn't really
bothered. I could just mess around and do the stupid things, and I
did. I wasn't really gobby [loud and insolent] but I was quite frowned
[upon] by the teachers and everything. And at the age of 13 you think
it's me against them. I was disruptive. I didn't really get bullied, I
wouldn't say—well, it's—I know I bullied other people. I wasn't
sexist about it; it was both boys and girls. I'd already made my mind
up. I knew I didn't need school. It's a bit of a regret now, for life and
everything.* ▪ Stephen, *United Kingdom*

For others it is the treatment by the teacher that leads to their withdrawal or deciding to leave:

I took keen interest in my studies [. . .] But one day our teacher, while checking our homework—I due to some reason failed to do my homework, along with four or five other class fellows—punished us corporally and abused us as well. I made a complaint to my parents and my father inquired of the teacher what was the good reason for abusing me. My father and teacher tried to reason it out, and my father took me out of study, and argued that teachers are not human. Now you will get admission in a madrassah [he said], where there are no abuses and you will live an ideal life with the scholars there.
        • Ehtesham, *Pakistan*

Even when the young person is in school, however, the school itself can act as a push or as a pull factor. The teachers may encourage the pupils to join, or the school system itself may be perceived as part of the apparatus of oppression:

One day in morning assembly at school our headmaster asked [told] us that Jihad broke out in Afghanistan. [He said to] make arrangements to join if anyone is interested. We group of five friends decided to join. • Ehtesham, *Pakistan*

It was the school that arranged the interview with the army.
        • Stephen, *United Kingdom*

If we were having an SRC meeting, the police would come around and shoot or beat the students. So many people died for the SRC. Even the government stimulated—encouraged—the vigilantes to kill the students. So it was these things that inspired us to join the revolution. • Benny, *South Africa*

We always had protests at school that time . . . some people were detained at that stage and they were detained for weeks sometimes or for months sometimes. • Kathryn, *South Africa*

Finally, some armies offer training and the possibility of obtaining qualifications as inducements:

The other thing I like about the army is the little perks it gives you. And looking back now, I knew, they told me that at the careers center as well. So that also got me keen to join 'cause I knew I could redo them [school exams] at any time, without any pressure.
        • Stephen, *United Kingdom*

Family and Friends

One of the crucial issues that emerges from this research is the role of the family: both as a push factor and as a pull factor in the decision of the young person to become involved. This comes up in every interview and in all dimensions, either as a direct or an indirect factor.

Although sometimes the whole family is involved in the armed group or in supporting the movement, more often, not all family members are involved, and not all the children join the armed forces or armed group. Age, gender, and position in the family are all factors, as well as the individual temperament and the specific relationships between siblings and between the specific child and one or both parents. This needs to be considered also in relation to demobilization and reintegration: where the young person's home life was very troubled, as well as when the family has ceased to exist, the received wisdom that the best interest of the demobilized child soldier is to be reunited with their family needs to be given further consideration.

Sometimes the situation within the family itself is the push factor, so that the young person is, in effect, running away from home. The emotional strains of family life are evident in many of the stories—both between parents and children, and when exacerbated by new relationships and step-siblings. In such circumstances, the armed groups in the conflict provide an escape route for the children:

My father is a fisherman, but he drank heavily. He used to come home drunk and beat all of us. Life at home was terrible. My mother went abroad to work in the Middle East as a housemaid. My home situation was unbearable. I had frequent quarrels with my father. I was often ridiculed as a useless person, especially when he was drunk. I hated going home and facing the insults of my father and I wanted to get out of that. ▪ Shutharsan, *Sri Lanka*

When I was younger, I was at school, and when I did some homework wrong, she'd [mother] whip me with the tape recorder flex and whack, she hit me, and I was like, ow! I used to run out of there crying and I, I said, no, I'm leaving, I'm getting out of here, and stuff like that. [. . .] What led me to join? I don't know, like the rejection, and like my family's indifference, and all that. I said to myself, no, how am I going to let myself be humiliated by my family? I can manage on my own, I know how to, and so I started hanging around with friends like that, like, and so then I was thinking about, every day I was thinking more and more about having guns and stuff like that and here I am. ▪ Richard, *Colombia*

My dad, I was seven years old when, once a . . . it was a public holiday and he came back drunk and that day he got us all together in the house and he killed himself. [. . .] we were all in a little room watching television and he arrived, he arrived and he kicked up a fuss and said no, he said that he was leaving, but he was going to take me with him, and so he arrived and he aimed at my head twice, but he didn't fire. [. . .] And then he got down on the ground, but he didn't fire either and when he pointed the gun here, at his temple, then he fired, and he fell there and he died. ▪ Otoniel, *Colombia*

Well, she's, she's [mother] left me black and blue. First she left me black and blue, then she says it makes her ashamed for people to say that her son is a thug—how about that?—she's like that. [. . .] I said to her, "If you're not going to understand me then it's better that I go, tell me to leave, I'm going." And so we often have arguments, and she says, "then go," and so she beats me and so it's best for me to keep quiet. I'm just like, "OK, mom; alright, mom," and like that, it's better, do you get me? You can't be, I mean, a mother can be really horrible but you can't ever . . . ▪ Carlos, *Colombia*

My dad died . . . and my mom, then, then she was going out with another man, she got married again, and that man he provided for us, didn't he, even though we weren't his children, but then the, the physical maltreatment we were given, I mean . . . [. . .] he beat us with a belt. I mean, he gave us everything but then he didn't stop reminding my mom about it, I mean, everything that he gave us. [. . .] I got fed up with my mom because everything that happened at home was always my fault or my sister's fault. [My mom beat me] sometimes with her slipper, or with a belt or something, and so, I started fighting with my mom [she starts to cry]. I got fed up with my mom and my granny took me in.
▪ Carolina, *Colombia,* referring to events at the age of 6

They beat me for playing up, playing up in the sense that I did something wrong, you know, bad things, and sometimes I didn't take any notice of what they were saying, and so my dad would beat me, he really laid into me, all the time; he used to beat me one time after another, several times in a row. And so I, well, I always got fed up with that, he hated me, he was always beating me, and so. . .
▪ Alfredo, *Colombia*

Sometimes it is not just the individual within the family, but the whole family that is perceived negatively (rightly or wrongly):

> *People haven't got a high opinion of us, no one likes us, because we're very, I mean, since we were little we've always been delinquents. We've always been crooks; since we were kids people told us, "Those kids aren't going to be friends with my children, they'll corrupt them." So, there, we were like, the rejected family, just leave them to it.* ▪ Richard, *Colombia*

The previous chapter considered family involvement in the military and/or the war as a general environmental factor, but it can also act at a more specific level:

> *I did not have any knowledge and experience of war and its aims, consequences, and that it may cause my death. I was just for supporting a member of my family, and for the sake of kinship relationship I joined to war.* ▪ Javad, *Afghanistan*

> *Well, I joined out of love for my brother [who had already joined], because I loved him a lot.* ▪ Jessica, *Colombia*

> *My cousins, well, now, now they're dead, they were killed two years ago. One of them, a cousin of mine who was involved a lot in the conflict, he used to show me lots of weapons, and he used to say that maybe when you grow up if I get killed then you can avenge me, and I used to say OK to everything, and I, and he taught me to use them [weapons], and all that stuff, and then when I was a little bit bigger, he was killed, not so long ago, about two years ago.*
> ▪ Richard, *Colombia*

> *My brother was a commander, he was a Liva, a military officer who can lead 2,000 soldiers. I joined my brother's forces.*
> ▪ Hassan, *Afghanistan*

> *My brother was lost for two to three months after he joined the conflict and the elders insisted we go after him and find some news of his whereabouts.* ▪ Aziz, *Pakistan*

> *My father is a warlord and his source of income is fighting and participation in combats. [. . .] It was in my mind from the beginning to become a commander like my father.* ▪ Khalid, *Pakistan*

> *My father was a warlord. [. . .] We were four children; three boys and me. [. . .] Yes, I was the last one. But I always wanted to be with my*

father [. . .] and then my brothers, they were with him also.
> ▪ Catherine, *DRC*

A recent ILO study[4] in the DRC found that none of the unrecruited children in their control group had a father in the armed forces, whereas 10 percent of the recruited children did. One interviewee listened to the discussions between his uncle and the "big brothers," the "old crocks," the veterans of the movement, when they were sitting around:

Because I was inquisitive, I could say that I wanted to know, "What does this represent?" And the more you get, the more you want to know. And I could not stop myself—I was in the thing.
> ▪ Solomon, *South Africa*

On my mom's side of the family, it's quite a big family. A lot of them were in the army as well and they'd send stuff to me. Even though I'd never met them, they were still interested, so I've had the army contact as well. So my family was very keen for me to join the army 'cause I was keen on it, basically.
> ▪ Stephen, *United Kingdom*

In other cases, the family can be the crucial factor in preventing the young person from joining, whether temporarily or permanently:

I did not take part in combat against the Americans because my father refused to allow me (I did not inform my father and my brothers even when I joined as a combatant [previously]). [. . .] If my father allows me I will definitely join to fight Jihad, otherwise if he refuses [I] will never join. ▪ Muhammad, *Pakistan*

It is important to realize the significance of parental influence in cases where many other vulnerability factors are in place. It strongly suggests that it is the decisive factor in keeping most young people from becoming involved in armed conflicts.

After family, their friends—the group they "hang out" with—are among the greatest influences on adolescents:

I had to leave the neighborhood, and then, then I went to live in San Jose; but over there, there were bad kids as well, and I started to get to know them and I started getting involved with guns and all that as well. [. . .] I arrived here when I was 14 years old, and the, well, I made some friends and through these friendships, then there were plans to include me in the group. We talked to the boss, and then I joined, I don't know [. . .] Well, first of all, because I was alone, and then with so many people having scores to settle with you, you need a bit of help. ▪ Andrés, *Colombia*

I joined the Guards because I had many friends there, they were my group of friends and they used to do guard duty. [. . .] that was like, the gang, to be in the Guards, and all that . . . my friends, my cousins, they all told me to join the Guards because that was great fun, so that I wasn't hanging around outside all the time, it's good to be doing something sometimes. ▪ Otoniel, *Colombia*

Three of us, me and my two friends, left for Afghanistan. We were young bloods; that's why we left very emotionally. Besides, [people returning from Afghanistan] used to tell about the current situation in Afghanistan. We were very curious about it so we left for Kabul.
▪ Aziz, *Pakistan*

Classmates, friends of the district—It's almost the majority of our youth who decided to join. ▪ Urbain, *DRC*

I became friends with some Cobras. Whenever they returned from battle, they would bring something back. I was always by their side asking them for something. I know a guy. [. . .] He said: "What are you doing here, I can tell that you are brave, you can hold a weapon, you know, once you try it will be fine." ▪ Albert, *Congo-Brazzaville*

It was almost like a mass movement. It was more influencing one another and those things. And it was not the thing of an individual. It was more a thing of the whole group does it, you know, so everyone does it. Because remember even at that time there was, for example, this scarf that the Palestinians are wearing—that red scarf. We used to wear that and anybody who was wearing was a student; it was a form of identification that you were actually a comrade or an activist, you know. ▪ Samuel, *South Africa*

I was busy with my religious education at a prominent madrassah, but as time passed, some of our friends decided to fight Jihad and together we left. ▪ Ehtesham, *Pakistan*

Well, when I was about 13, my best mate, this old boy, the same age as me and lived 100 meters down the road: even though he was at a different school from me, in the nighttime we used to do everything together, going to Cadets, going out on the weekend, drinking and smoking and everything. I tried getting him in the army but because of his medical background, like, in the head and everything, he couldn't actually get in. I went on leave last August in the middle of a Northern Ireland tour, a six-monther. And about four days after I'd gone back, he went to prison for stabbing someone. Like I said, I was always with him at that time. I had to get out of that. He was my best mate. I'm still in contact with him now but I wouldn't really class him as my best mate. ▪ Stephen, *United Kingdom*

I always wanted to join but I don't know if I had the motivation about me to do it. My mate was going for the army as well, at the new school, and he requested that he wanted an interview to speak to someone about the army. And he said to me, "Yeah, you're in Cadets as well, can you make that two." I tagged along to it. I went to a few interviews over the months [. . .] and it all progressed from there really. It was really my mate who was interested. Because I was in Cadets and he pulled me along with it. ▪ Andrew, *United Kingdom*

The development of a conscious identity, both as an individual and as part of a group, is also an important part of the process of growing up, and thus makes a particular appeal to adolescents. The awareness of the respected status of those who are involved, and of an enhanced personal status once one has joined is appealing:

I feel loyal. [. . .] Proud. Proud to defend my people.
▪ David, *Northern Ireland*

Everyone down here is basically proud of what I am, proud of who I am. ▪ Paul, *Northern Ireland*

I always go back bragging every time I see them [friends]. Normally the one I come out with is "I'm getting paid now." [. . .] my girlfriend [is] envious of places I've been, what I've done and all that type of stuff. I'm sure some of my other friends are as well because I've got my own car, I got my driving license through the army. I'm in the process of getting my own house, obviously with my girlfriend. And most of my mates aren't capable of being able to do that.
▪ Andrew, *United Kingdom*

I liked the idea of doing things at a young age that you couldn't do on Civvy Street [in civilian life], ya'know? [. . .] General things: like you couldn't exactly walk around London with a weapon, could you? Whether it's real or not. Whereas in the army, and I was in my

*uniform—if I was carrying a weapon people would turn a blind eye,
wouldn't they. Little things like that. And especially as a teenager,
look at the police, you got to be at least 21 to join the police, then you
have to go on specialist training and everything. [. . .] I haven't taken
drugs for three years, more than that, three and a half years. I'm not
disruptive. I'm quite polite now. I've completely sorted my life out.
Before, I'd be down at the pub and everything. People used to know
what I was like, vandalism and everything; they've actually got a
little bit more respect for me. I know how to behave myself.*
▪ Stephen, *United Kingdom*

The Military/Parties to the Conflict

Many armies (and armed groups) recognize the appeal of status and uniforms and actively seek to attract young people. In developed countries
this often happens through schools, cadet programs, displays, advertising, and recruitment offices. In the United Kingdom (and many other
Western countries) the cadet programs offered to young people are
designed to stimulate interest in a career in the armed forces.[5] On its
website, the British Ministry of Defence states: "The Cadets, which we
support both financially and materially, help to keep young people in
touch with the Armed Forces. They involve over 130,000 young people
aged between 12 and 22, supervised by 23,000 volunteer adults, in more
than 3,000 cadet units."[6]

This strategy clearly works in some cases:

*I joined Cadets when I was 13. And then I joined the regular army as
soon as I could. When I was in the Cadets, I became aware of the
possibility to join the army. There was a lot of talk in the Cadets, and
I'd seen leaflets and flyers all over the place.*
▪ Stephen, *United Kingdom*

Active youth recruitment comes from armed groups as well as from the
armed forces:

*I used to see the LTTE soldiers come into the area I lived. [. . .] I used
to see them at the crossroad junctions. Sometimes they call for new
recruits. They used to describe the bad things done by the Sinhala
people and sometimes showed videos of attacks, and we were thrilled*

to watch these. At the end they ask for volunteers. I was drawn to them and wanted to join them. ▪ Ajith, *Sri Lanka*

Other young people initiate the contact themselves, but are then encouraged to join:

Once I met a soldier. I was just walking around, he was walking as well; I was curious, I wanted to know him. [. . .] I told him that I would come to see him the following day. I was very glad to have spoken with him. He was beautiful! He and his uniform! [. . .] Strong! He was beautiful and well built, he had a beautiful color, and he was brown. The following day, I left over there. [. . .] He sent me to buy cigarettes for him. They started to tell stories of soldiers. I was there! Later on, I asked him what I would have to do if I wanted to be a soldier. He said to me: "Hey, we're looking for children like you who want to do everything for their country!" He told me things! [. . .] He explained to me how to leave, he directed me. I told him that I would come. ▪ Germain, *DRC*

Photo by T. Voeten

Violent heroes (such as Che Guevara) have a strong influence

In addition to general youth recruitment, sometimes it is specifically targeted at a particular young person, linked to an event or to the person's perceived availability:

> *I learned much through the Tiger information. My uncle was killed by the army [. . .] Although we were told this we did not know definitely who killed him or how he really died. But the Tigers convinced us. I was very angry. Everyone in the family wanted revenge. I was more convinced that it was my duty by the family honor to take revenge. I was a person who was not much concerned about the war. Tiger recruiters convinced and changed my way of thinking to take revenge.* ▪ Sabesan, *Sri Lanka*

Some of them actively seek to make contact without waiting to be approached either generally or specifically:

> *I always approached the organization and let them know I was prepared. To die. But they knew I was prepared anyway.*
> ▪ David, *Northern Ireland*

> *I wasn't really told about it. I found out about the army purely because I wanted to be in the army. I put myself out of my own way to find out about it. Once I looked in the Yellow Pages, found the army and I just asked several questions.* ▪ Andrew, *United Kingdom*

Some had a good perception of the group they were joining:

> *I joined this group because it's very serious, they teach you to behave, they have a good appearance, seriousness, no bad habits, and so I liked this group best.* ▪ Andrés, *Colombia*

The other side of the coin is when the behavior of one side provokes the impulse to join the other side:

> *I planned to run away from this terrible situation of forced hard-labor work without payment for the army. As I was the only son I knew that my mother was going to feel very sad. I was kind of torn between the two situations of being at home and getting harassed every day or running away to fight for a useful cause. I had to be free so I decided to join LTTE who were fighting against this type of situation. I was being harassed and tormented to work for nothing, and this was a terrible situation for me.* ▪ Sathiyan, *Sri Lanka*

What also made me also join at that stage—like, you know, the police—the police visits to our houses. The threat that they used to give, you know, and the way they used to wake you up at night— they used to shine a torch in your face just to see who you are and question you and things like that. And that gave me more of a determination to go in that, you know, and to see what can be done to make a change to our society. ▪ Kathryn, South Africa

Sometimes the military rob the family of their means of survival:

Mom gave me her coins and loincloths, I went to the market. While going to the market, some Cobras stopped me. They were armed; they said that they needed to get back my goods. ▪ Henri, Congo

Sometimes it is the threat to the security of the family or individual members of it:

My father was tired of political conflicts and was not active. But the Taliban put him in prison; first because he is a Tajik, secondly he had liberal motivations and thoughts. [. . .] He already was arrested, and

For many children, violence is just around the corner

he had been in jail for two months. But because he had made no mistakes, the Taliban released him. [. . .] When he was released he began to support Shah Masoud. Then the Taliban arrested him and sent him to jail in Kandahar. ▪ Mustafa, *Afghanistan*

The murdering of my family. [. . .] My father was a loyalist leader. [He was shot] at my mother's front door. [It was done by someone] from another paramilitary organization. ▪ David, *Northern Ireland*

Aye, well my cousin, he wasn't out rioting, he was walking along the street and then he got set upon by a group, and I just don't like that at all. That's why I go out and riot, because I'm not going to let people, and even the police, because they're heavy-handed when they're coming in. They come in and start beating people for nothing, and all this. And they usually come in heavy-handed and so you have to riot with them. [. . .] Then after the Shankill bombing, that was just another thing that put me to join the UYM [Ulster Young Militants]. [. . .] My ma was just out of the UDA headquarters at the time it happened. She was about 10 or 20 feet away from it at the time it exploded. And I thought she was dead that day, I was told she was dead and I was crying and all. And I got up and she was, she was there. ▪ Michael, *Northern Ireland*

My uncle was a regular soldier; he was chief sergeant in the army; he was killed by the Ninjas in '98. He was my only uncle from my mother's side. His death totally destabilized me. I needed revenge. You know, he was an important person in our family.
▪ François, *Congo-Brazzaville*

Politics and Identity

Rather than family or friends, it may be an issue of group identity or political ideology that either calls for, or demands, the participation of young people. It must be stressed that identity issues are sensitive to manipulation for political ends. Creating the idea of a common identity, whether based on religion, race, tribe, ethnicity, or other factors, is a common ploy in identifying the "other" as the enemy to be opposed:

There I met some members of the movement who had been pestering me since I was 12 years to join them; they asked me to come with

*them. They said it is for our people, and we all have to sacrifice.
Anyway, they had been telling me about all the terrible things that
have happened to our people and how bad the Sinhala people are.*
                                        ▪ Shutharsan, *Sri Lanka*

Although it seems clear from Shutharsan's description that he joined as
the result of a prolonged campaign of political and ethnic indoctrina-
tion, the immediate trigger for his joining was an imminent beating
from his father, as is quoted in the next chapter.

*That Father was always trying to teach us the thing that is
happening, we must do this, this and this. We must do these things,
to fight the apartheid system. So all the time they pressured us and
then they gave us the thing to . . . That Father was changing my
mind so much, just because he was convincing me—a lot.*
                                        ▪ Malcolm, *South Africa*

*I could see that there was no justice in this country. There was no
justice. So I foresaw the reason for me to be really active, more than
before.* ▪ Benny, *South Africa*

*I did worry about the national situation. [. . .] I only gradually
became aware of the great destruction due to the war. I realized that
people were dying, houses were being destroyed, and the military was
fighting. I was told that all the destruction was because of the army.
I felt strongly that it was all unwanted destruction, and I wanted to
stop it all.* ▪ Sabesan, *Sri Lanka*

Many of the young people have been exposed to ideas and images
that make the idea of fighting attractive to them. Sometimes this is
directly related to other factors, such as status, or fulfilling a religious
calling, but it can also be the more general appeal for adolescents of
adventure, excitement, heroism, and emulating the role models presented either directly or through films, stories, or other images. Having
experienced the reality of war, many of them reflect how different that
reality was from their previous image of it:

*Though I planned to join the combat, [. . .] personally, I was curious
about the climatic conditions. [. . .] We reached there at a time when
grapes were ripened and we enjoyed different types of seasonal fruit.
They [the Taliban] gave us a Kalashnikov for security and we kept it*

for security purposes, though later on joined as combatants, but that was not our priority. Our interest was a recreational visit.

■ Muhammad, *Pakistan*

We didn't know about the whole reality of exile, what we were going to be confronted with. Because I guess initially it was, it was shocking. ■ Samuel, *South Africa*

I didn't see all that, I didn't know that in the army I would suffer. I didn't think of the suffering. When we saw a soldier, we used to say that he got a job, it's money too. We didn't know what happened in the army. We only saw from behind. ■ Germain, *DRC*

We were very happy to travel in their Pajero [four-wheel-drive jeep]. At that time of my life I did not know about war. [. . .] I used to see the LTTE soldiers come into the area I lived. They were very smartly dressed in uniforms. I used to admire them with the buttons and nicely polished guns. They go about in big cars and carry big guns. [. . .] I was drawn to them and wanted to join them.

■ Ajith, *Sri Lanka*

I went to war because I wanted to see how it was. When you are in the camp, you see people who leave to the front line, and they sing.

■ Catherine, *DRC*

You know the little ones when they see you, they run after you, they look at you; they want to be just like you. ■ Pierre, *Congo-Brazzaville*

From childhood, I liked guns. All the children play with guns and if they can't buy one, they make one with wood. At first, in training, we were given wooden guns—I did not like that, I wanted the real ones that kill. I wanted to fight and die for a cause. But it was only after joining that I learned about the real cause. ■ Gajathukan, *Sri Lanka*

The guerrillas used to pass through the hamlet, and I used to look at them, and well, I thought, wow, those guns, they must be able to shoot a long way, and as I really liked going hunting, so I thought that one of those guns must be able to shoot further than a normal rifle, and so I asked my dad and my dad said, of course, one of those could shoot really far, and so they came by one, and I, like, wanted to join them, but I wasn't sure, and so for a while I couldn't make up my mind. ■ Alfredo, *Colombia*

When I left to confront the Northern Alliance, [. . .] it was considered religious duty to fight against the Northern Alliance. [. . .] Then we [three of us] managed to reach there but observed that they [Northern Alliance] were also raising slogans of "Allah-O-Akbar" [Allah is Great] before opening fire just like us. After continuously fighting for one year, we realized that Muslims are confronting and killing each other. This is not the concept of Jihad, thus we decided to demobilize and returned home. [. . .] I liked the aspect of patrolling in the city in latest-model vehicles, a Kalashnikov hanging over the shoulder, visiting new places, it was so adventurous. Just like a dream come true, here we dreamed to be a soldier and being in Afghanistan our dream came true. Many more joined for the lust to enjoy this status but lost their lives.
▪ Aziz, *Pakistan*

In the United Kingdom, the Cadet forces are used to give young people an attractive idea of what army life is all about:

Just a general question about what your experience of being in the Cadets was like.
Me and my mates had a good laugh. Just chilled out and everything. I enjoyed playing around with the guns and stuff like that. ▪ Stephen, *United Kingdom*

Do you think the Cadets gave you a realistic feel for what army life is like?
Yes, much of the things are the same. Things like a muster parade. Most mornings, you'd form up outside and they would call a roll, a register, to find out if everyone's there. Another thing is the meal timings. Having to be at a certain place at the right time. It's learning self-discipline as well. If you did something wrong, you'd either get a slap for doing it or would get shouted at or made to run somewhere or punished. ▪ Andrew, *United Kingdom*

But army life, nevertheless, is not the same:

The Cadet experience can be a little help with the basic training, but apart from that it did not really. The army was a completely new job.

The Cadets, it's a hobby, while the army, it's your profession. [. . .] I knew there'd be discipline. Physical fitness is important. I knew that it would be interesting and that I'd get buzzes every now and again like when I'm doing section attack, like firing my weapons system, ya'know. In Cadets you could only do a certain amount—obviously safety—we were only little teenagers and everything.
▪ Stephen, *United Kingdom*

Conclusion

While Chapter 1 identified the key factors without which young people are unlikely to become involved with armed forces or armed groups, this chapter has looked at what impacts more directly on the individual young person. Although war in general creates vulnerability, more specifically it puts individuals and their families at risk physically and threatens their means of survival both in terms of food and financially. The army or armed group fills this gap or promises to do so. Allied to these elements are the presence or absence of schooling, and whether the school is used physically, culturally, or psychologically as a recruiting ground. The role of schools illustrates the dual nature of some of the factors: being out of school (whether through one's own actions or by *force majeure*) leaves young people vulnerable to recruitment, especially if they cannot find employment or other economically viable activities. At the same time, some schools may encourage recruitment by allowing the army or the armed group access to students, presenting them as good options, or as being the fulfilment of ethnic, religious, or political imperatives. Some specific young people may be targeted, whether in or out of school, as being perceived by the potential recruiter as likely material because of age, sex, availability, aptitude, vulnerability, or for other reasons.

In a similar way, the family can be the cause of recruitment because one of its members is alienated or ill-treated, or because the family (or a key member of it) is currently or traditionally involved in the armed forces or group or aligned in a way that encourages or provides approval to such involvement.

For a young person who is in trouble, at home, at school, or elsewhere, and who is seeking support, status, a sense of personal identity and role at a critical time in their own physical, emotional, and societal development, the armed forces or armed group can seem an attractive option, particularly where such involvement is condoned or encouraged by the society or culture, and/or by key influences at home, at school, or within their peer group.

What remains is one question: What is it that for specific individuals tips the balance from being in an at-risk or vulnerable situation, thinking about joining perhaps, and actually acting on it? This is the subject of Chapter 3.

Notes

1. The concept of "military age" is well recognized in practice, though it has fluid boundaries. International law prohibits any recruitment or use in hostilities of children under 15 years. Children who are or appear to be approaching this age are therefore often targeted. The reality is that this means that children of 13 upwards are often viewed as approaching military age—depending on their size and physical development, which is, of course, subject to considerable individual variation.

2. In the United Kingdom, rates of pay range from £16.85 daily for under-17s up to £29.42 daily for those over 17 and a half (Amnesty International 2000).

3. The failure to fulfill promises of payment, schools, and better conditions leads not only to a general disillusionment in many cases, but can present specific problems in relation to demobilization. Dumas and de Cock (2003) found that some young people are reluctant to be demobilized because they have not been paid what they were promised.

4. Dumas and de Cock 2003, p. 31.

5. Amnesty International 2000.

6. www.mod.uk/aboutus/factfiles/community.htm (consulted on 05 May 2003).

3

The Critical Moment

The general setting (the environment) and the more specific situation of the particular young person are factors in determining their involvement in warfare. However, many young people who share these characteristics still do not get involved. In no situation do all children, or even all adolescents, become soldiers, even if they are in a war zone, impoverished, have broken families, are unemployed, and not in school. What is the crucial factor that makes the difference? Some of these young people admit that they had thought about the possibility of joining for years. Others had never thought about it. Remember that these are not the youngest children; nor are they the ones who were abducted by the fighting forces. They are adolescents who define themselves as volunteers. How much real choice existed will be considered in Chapter 6. Here, insofar as the young soldiers and ex-soldiers themselves were able or willing to do so, the critical moment of making the decision or responding to events is identified.

Outbreak of Violence

I wouldn't have joined if the cease-fire hadn't been broke[n], so I wouldn't. ▪ Michael, *Northern Ireland*

Most of the young people do not decide to go and look for a war to fight. They simply find themselves in the place where the conflict is taking place:

Until the Taliban took power I never seriously attended in the wars. [. . .] The Taliban [. . .] were foreigners and I wanted to defend my

country against the foreigners. So, in 1994 I entered in war [. . .] the Taliban came into Mazarsharif and we wanted to defend our city.
▪ Hassan, *Afghanistan*

We were living in our home in the city of Mazar when the Taliban attacked us. [. . .] Then we began to fight with the Taliban. [. . .] we had to fight them. [. . .] When the Taliban surrounded us and our family and children, we could not sleep and we were worried and scared. [. . .] We were in an insecure state; even in our homes we were not secure. So we decided to guard our home at night. Then every area and alley created a group of local security guards. This local police was comprised of people of each alley; in fact every family had to send a person, we named him Payledar, to the local guard group. [. . .] we were armed. I always carried a gun. [. . .] Some nights I was Payledar and some nights my father, and sometimes my brothers. ▪ Mortaza, *Afghanistan*

Of course, some families have taken evasive action in order to protect their children from precisely these problems. They relocate to another part of the country, or go abroad—or send their children away for education. However, the families who can and do act in this way will tend to be those who have the financial means, who do not come from a military tradition, and who are a functioning unit. This illustrates the way in which the different vulnerability factors interrelate.

Lack of Income/Poverty

The critical loss of means of livelihood, taking away immediate means for survival, can be the trigger to join:

The Iranian government asked and forced Afghani refugees in Iran to go back to Afghanistan. The shopkeeper that I was working in his shop sold his shop and left Iran. To support me, the shopkeeper introduced me to an Afghani military and political group in Mashhahad. I had to work with that group because I had no other way and there was no other option for me.
▪ Javad, *Afghanistan*

Sometimes, the need to protect and support their family reaches a crisis of such urgency that the only solution seems to be to sign up immediately with the armed forces or armed groups:

Anonymous

War is part of the normal everyday environment

When I returned, I found my sister; she felt so bad, and I didn't have the means of treating her. There I knew that I was going to take up the weapon to feed my family, because at this time I knew that the Ninjas gave some manioc [cassava, a starchy root eaten as a staple food] to their recruits. They even gave money. I couldn't do anything else; I was forced to take the weapon to help, to save my family.
▪ Henri, Congo-Brazzaville

I signed up to protect my sisters, because a lot of boys attacked girls, women, and mothers. My brother was not around, he had fled the village. I had to pay [. . .] to stop the militaries from taking my sister. Then I had a sister that was pregnant, so we needed the money.
▪ Albert, Congo-Brazzaville

School

The sudden loss of school may precipitate the decision to join up:

When I was still at school, in my last year, I was going to the army interviews because they said I could do it. However, they wouldn't

accept me until I left school officially. I got expelled [from school] at
the end of year 10 when I was 15. ▪ Stephen, *United Kingdom*

Conversely, school may be the specific recruiting ground, as at the broader level. Where the armed group runs or has access to the schools (as with the LTTE in Sri Lanka), or where inspirational religious figures are brought in to motivate the students, it is hard to resist:

While being at madrassah a young boy named "Noor Muhammad"
used to visit us and deliver speeches that fighting shoulder to
shoulder with the Taliban is Jihad. It made us very emotional, that
if he, Noor Muhammad, can join, why can't we? We consulted one
of our Maulvis [clergy] and asked about our possibility of going for
Jihad. He replied that it was the most suitable time to fight Jihad
under the flag of the Taliban. We were still reluctant but the
repeated visits of Noor Muhammad and his speeches brainwashed
us to the extent that I began to think that if he, Noor Muhammad,
more handsome than me, is ready to sacrifice his life, why can't I?
Then one day Noor Muhammad, along with his companions, called
upon us and said that they were planning to leave for Afghanistan
and avail the chance of fighting side-by-side with Noor
Muhammad. We also decided to accompany them.
▪ Ehtesham, *Pakistan*

Family Events

As already noted, the family is one of the most important elements for any young person. The family situation, including economics, education, values, and geographic location, are significant environmental factors, as are how the family sees its role in society, and in relation to the conflict, and how others perceive it and its members. More immediate and specific is the question of how the family functions internally; whether it is cohesive and supportive of its members, or whether it is divided emotionally or physically through death, divorce, separation, or other factors. It is hardly surprising that for many young people, family events are the catalyst for their decision to join the armed forces or armed group.

Sometimes the catastrophic loss in the conflict of all or most of the immediate family precipitates the decision to join:

*I first knew about the war when my father was killed. [. . .] So
I joined. There was nothing else I could do then. [. . .] I joined
willingly because I did not have anybody to encourage me. [. . .]
My first reaction was to take revenge and kill many soldiers who
attacked our village at that time who had killed my father [. . .] by
that time the high school was burnt, all of my belongings burnt
down, no education for me again, and my mother was ill and
abandoned in our house and died, so I thought that I can never be a
human being again. That's why I joined them. [. . .] I didn't have
anybody in the world. No mother, no brother, no father.*

■ Momoh, *Sierra Leone*

A similar case is described in harrowing detail in Sayanathen's vignette
at the end of this chapter.

In other instances the loss might not have been so catastrophic, but
the urge for revenge caused an immediate reaction:

*When we received the message of my brother's martyrdom to avail the
opportunity which Almighty Allah had provided, to perform the duty,
we decided to join and left for Afghanistan. [His father had died when
he was one year old, and his brother's death left him as the eldest].
We were young and immature, that's why we decided to join without
consulting anyone. It was easy to cross the border without any
hindrance.* ■ Aziz, *Pakistan*

I thought my father had been killed; I was like an injured lion.

■ Pascal, *Congo-Brazzaville*

Many young people run away from abusive or exploitative home
situations into the armed forces or armed groups. This is true for both
boys and girls. The general descriptions by Alfredo (Colombia) and
Shutharsan (Sri Lanka) of their unhappy family experiences were
quoted in Chapter 2. They and Carolina (Colombia) recall vividly the
precise incident that crystallized the general situation into a trigger to
run away and join up:

*No, the day that my mom beat me was when, I mean, when I made
that decision. [. . .] I joined the FARC because I was fed up with my
mom . . . well, my mom had already told me off, and she'd told me
that she was going to hit me again, and so I thought that she was*

going to beat me again, and so these, these guerrillas appeared, to do guard duty, and I met up with them on the corner. I talked to one of them and they said, OK, they would pick me up in a park at eight o'clock that night, they told me to pack up a bag with a blanket and nothing else, they said that there they would give me everything else, and so I went there and they took me with them. ▪ Carolina, *Colombia*

So one day I was working there, and my dad was angry at me. And the truth is: well, my dad had to go and get some firewood, and so I went to work for an uncle. I was there when some guerrillas came by, and so I went and talked to them, and I wanted to join them. [. . .] After that [discussion], I went back home—they told me just to take a bag and toothbrush—so I went back home and I took that and I went off with them. ▪ Alfredo, *Colombia*

One day, my father [. . .] was looking for me to beat me with a stick— he was drunk. I had gone fishing and I heard it from someone. There I met some members of the movement [LTTE] who had been pestering me since I was 12 years to join them, and they asked me to come with them. They said it is for our people, and we all have to sacrifice. Anyway they had been telling me about all the terrible things that have happened to our people and how bad the Sinhala people are. I was thinking about joining them from [when I was] 12 years old and this was the ideal time to join. My father will never dare come to the Tiger camps looking for me. ▪ Shutharsan, *Sri Lanka*

Others go to join family members who are already in the group:

When he [her brother] got to the house, I was called for: "Your brother needs you." So I said, "Well, what's this about?" He said, "I've come for you," and I went. No more. I liked that and I wanted to get out of there. ▪ Jessica, *Colombia*

It was 1991 and I was studying at school when I made up my mind to visit my father during the summer vacations. He was "Coomandaar" [Commander] leading a faction at Kunhar, Afghanistan. [. . .] When I reached there war broke out accidentally the same day. I was just ten year old at that time. [. . .] I was very horrified for the first two days and in confusion ran here and there; I fired a bullet or two and returned to my original position. [. . .] They made fun of me and advised me to leave but I insisted on remaining there and thus accompanied them. [. . .] I also accompanied my father and confronted the Northern Alliance on various front lines, but I was interested to remain close to my father and fight under his supervision. ▪ Khalid, *Pakistan*

Yet others are thinking about joining for a while and it is the encouragement and support of their family that pushes them to take the step:

They were quite supportive about it. [. . .]. My dad took time off work to take me to the careers center and everything, so I was happy with that. He encouraged me that it would sort me out, which it has done.
▪ Stephen, *United Kingdom*

Friends

The influence of the peer group during adolescence is very apparent. Frequently, rather than being an individual decision to join, it is two or more friends who go together. Sometimes one is clearly the leader, sometimes it is more of a sense that "go one, go all":

At an occasion when we were all seated on the ground, my Talib friend told that "Mammu"—he used to call me Mamma or Uncle— "we are joining them, OK?" I responded that we were not skilled in combat and might get injured. He said, "OK, then you stay here. I am leaving with them [Taliban] for the fight." I argued, "It would be unjust that you die here and I return home safely. Let's join together." ▪ Muhammad, *Pakistan*

There were many students, but the day when we left it was only myself and a guy called "X." And there was the whole issue of which party we were going to join. X wanted to join the Black Consciousness Movement. He was actually the one who told us that the Consciousness Movement is the one of the PAC. And that is how it went. ▪ Samuel, *South Africa*

Recruitment

It sometimes happens that the recruiting activities of the armed forces or the armed group catch the young person at the precise moment when he or she is ready to join. Carlos (Colombia) was in a prison for young offenders for having killed someone, and joined as soon as he was released:

*They talked to me, and they said join right away, and so right away
. . . and I, I didn't think about it. Straight away, I went to see one of
the "jobs." [. . .] Yes, straight away, and without thinking about it.*
                                                        ▪ Carlos, *Colombia*

*I was already mobilized in my mind, when Kabila arrived with
his Rwandan allies. He organized a meeting at Bukavu and made
promises to the young people. I was approached very easily, with my
friends, we didn't hesitate, and we joined. [. . .] I was eleven years
old.* ▪ Joseph, *DRC*

*To become a priest, much work was needed; we needed many good
marks and morals too. However, what stopped me, it's the Release,[1]
as the Release arrived, almost all the young people left. In a class of
fifty pupils, the day of the Release, you found only twelve pupils in
the room. [. . .] It's the same day that I joined the army, our president
held an official meeting. He asked the young people, the pupils, to
come to support him in the army. All those who loved him could send
their child into the army, it was his message. [. . .] Therefore, I left.*
                                                        ▪ Urbain, *DRC*

*We didn't ask anything; but when they came to the meeting, they said
that they wanted the small seminarists. At the beginning, they said
that they were going to protect us; then they said that we would have
good things. All that pushed us to be in the army.* ▪ Michel, *DRC*

*Another estate was just above us, a UDA estate: we went up there,
went into a house. I says to them I want to join up; he says, "Right,
call back in about ten minutes." So we sat for about ten minutes
round the corner and I went back round and walked down. And when
I went in, there was a boy standing there with a balaclava and a gun.*
                                                        ▪ Paul, *Northern Ireland*

*When I was first told that he was cut up into pieces by the Muslims,
I felt anger at those who had killed my father. I was generally the
quiet type and I used to think on my own, and the more I thought
about how my father was killed the more angry I was. I wanted to do
the same to them. I used to get bouts of anger and I was angry with
everyone, including myself, especially for not being able to do
anything to take revenge. [. . .] I ran away from home and joined the
LTTE. I joined again on one of the sudden impulses I used to get the
same year [end 2001], when I thought of my father. It was my duty
and mission in life to take revenge.* ▪ Gajathukan, *Sri Lanka*

As the last quotation illustrates, although some young people talk about wanting revenge in personal terms, it is not always clear how much this is really their own personal feelings (at least initially) and how much revenge is a construct of society or of adults using the young person's anger, despair, frustration, and abandonment to fuel a commitment to "revenge" or "avenge" in the name of the group or the cause. Sometimes the recruiters deliberately tell the young person that a relative has been killed, or that the other side was responsible for a relative's death, to encourage them to join up or to motivate them to take "revenge":

> *One of my friends was shot in his head because he refused to join them [the AFRC]. He was killed right in front of me.*
>
> ▪ Arthur, *Sierra Leone*

Conclusion

Some of the adolescents interviewed could identify a specific moment or event that precipitated their decision to join an armed force or armed group. For a young person witnessing the massacre of their family, the nature and suddenness of the event leaves little room for other factors. However, even in these circumstances, joining an armed group only becomes the option because the group and the conflict exist. If the destruction of the family had occurred in peacetime because, say, they had been involved in a traffic accident, the response would have been different. Thus the existence of the war, and the fact that an armed party to the conflict committed the massacre, are relevant as well as the absolute loss of family.

More often, the young person has already been considering the possibility of joining up. The degree of seriousness of this consideration may vary. However, the scene is set and the event identified is the one that tipped the balance from thought to action. Often this is a specific example of the factors that have already started the thought process: for example, another beating or expectation of one imminently from a parent, or the absence of parents at a critical moment when the soldiers are present and are encouraging the young person to go with them. Thus the "trigger" often is not an isolated event so much as a specific moment in a chain of interrelated factors that have cumulatively put the young person at risk. At the same time, it is important to recognize that the nature of adolescence makes them particularly vulnerable to making decisions impulsively and without necessarily weighing all the factors or considering the long-term implications of their decisions.

Many of the factors identified are negative ones: push factors involving home, school, the economic situation, insecurity, and so on. At the same time, pull factors encourage the decision not merely to run away, or the need to find food, shelter, security, financial support, and so on, but to seek it with the armed forces or the armed group rather than elsewhere.

VIGNETTE: SAYANATHEN, A BOY FROM SRI LANKA, JOINED THE LTTE AT 11 YEARS OLD

One day my father and my elder brother were taken away for questioning by the army. That was a terrible time. My father (I came to know later) was hit till his jaw joint got dislocated. At the time, when my father and brother were not in the house, the soldiers came and called out. I was watching when my mother came out, my younger sister too came out with her. The soldiers then shot at my mother point-blank and both my mother and my sister died on the spot. As my father and brother were taken away they did not know anything about the deaths of my mother and sister at that time.

My elder sister and I buried my mother and my sister in our garden. We dug the grave by ourselves with our bare hands. That will not go away from my mind. At that time, I was only 11 years old. The killing of my mother and my little sister that happened before my eyes made me decide to join the LTTE immediately and I made up my mind to take revenge. I did not tell anyone. My father and brother were released after some time. As my father came back he was very sad and decided to take us away to another area he thought was safe for us. He thought we could forget everything if we left the place. I will never ever forget this till I die. I did not want to go with him. There were so many children without parents. I could not think of anything else.

I wanted to kill those killers who kill the innocent children and their parents. Otherwise, I thought all the children would be killed or their parents would be killed and they would have to be orphans.

I joined the movement on my own. I went out alone from Madhu to Mannar and found out where they were and went and joined them. Later my sister also had taken the decision to join the LTTE. I supported her decision, and others who wanted to join the movement.

If I had not joined the movement I would have been unhappy. How can you allow those who kill children and innocent mothers to go scot-free? I wanted to kill, take revenge for all that I went through. My father and brother were taken away, and they came and shot my mother and little sister. I loved them so much. My family, a nice happy family, was destroyed. With my bare hands, crying so much, my sister and I dug the grave for my mother and sister. We were just small children. Now I can tell you that I grew up overnight. I became like a big person and I took the decision to join the LTTE. I was very angry and wanted to take revenge.

Note

1. The "Release" was the moment when the rebels went into the villages and actively reached out to children and their parents, when they were rallying for support before starting their march toward Kinshasa.

4

A Complex of Risk Factors

The previous chapters have brought together the words of young soldiers and ex-soldiers, and from these we have gone some way toward identifying three levels of influence—environmental, the specific situation of the adolescent, and the immediate trigger for involvement—on the actions of these young people. In this chapter we will draw these results together, and try to find the linkages between the factors themselves and with existing research. First, however, we present the full story of one young ex-soldier, Javad. By close analysis of his story we draw common factors from individual experience, and illustrate how these elements operate and interact in real life.

Javad's Story

Javad is 20 years old. He is from Afghanistan and lives in the Islamic Republic of Iran. His story illustrates clearly the many war-related events and decisions that ultimately led to his involvement in armed conflict. Growing up in an environment of oppression, poverty, and disrupted family life, his ambitions were not to become a fighter, but the lack of other opportunities runs like a red thread throughout his story. The trigger factors for his decision to join up were the sudden loss of income, returning to his home village and finding that war was all around him, a family member who was involved, and a group with a shared ideology. This annotated example shows the complex accumulation of factors and the dynamic interrelationship between them that epitomizes so many of these young people's decisions to join an armed group.

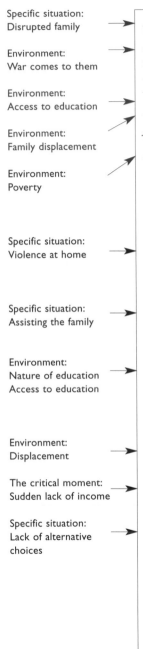

Specific situation:
Disrupted family

Environment:
War comes to them

Environment:
Access to education

Environment:
Family displacement

Environment:
Poverty

Specific situation:
Violence at home

Specific situation:
Assisting the family

Environment:
Nature of education
Access to education

Environment:
Displacement

The critical moment:
Sudden lack of income

Specific situation:
Lack of alternative
choices

I was around age eight or nine when I lost my father. When the Russians bombarded an area called Garma, which is near our region. [. . .] Three or four years after my father's death, one of my uncles who had migrated to Iran in the early years of the revolution came back to Afghanistan. [. . .] He remained for about one year. In 1989, in order to learn modern education, I came to Iran with my uncle. [. . .] I was a teenage boy without my family and alone. My uncle was very poor and he just received some little money from his seminary that didn't afford his own life expenditure. [. . .] Half of the day I worked and another half I went to school. I did work at carpet weaving and hosiery and dealing socks. I had to be self-sufficient economically. In order to not be a burden on my uncle's life and his family. [. . .] Despite that I was able to manage myself, my uncle's wife made many troubles for me. [. . .] She hated me and several times tortured and hit me. In the night I didn't have bedclothes; I had just a small blanket so that if I put it on my head then my feet would be left out and if I covered my feet my head remained uncovered. At the same time, I didn't want to tell my mother my problems, because I knew my mother was not able to help me and she could not do anything for me except that if I told her it just would make her very sad and worry.

Then I asked my uncle to send me to another place. I requested him to send me to a religious school among seminarians, then I would study, and my uncle's wife would become happier. He accepted. [. . .] After one week I couldn't pay money for food. And then other seminarians forced me to leave there. I became homeless.

[Javad was given a job by a fellow countryman, but in 1993 the Iranian government asked and forced Afghan refugees in Iran to go back to Afghanistan.] *The shopkeeper that I was working for sold his shop and left Iran. To support me, the shopkeeper introduced me to an Afghani military and political group in Mashhahad. I had to work with that group because I had no other way and there was no other option for me. So, in 1993 I began to work for that group [. . .] the Hezbollah. Hezbollah had a magazine called* Zohur. *My job was to gather news and information for that magazine. I must listen to radios and collect news about Afghanistan. I must record all news and transcribe them and edit and provide them for publications. [. . .] I slept nights in the office of the group, because I did not have any place, and on days I worked there for them. [. . .] In 1995 our group moved to Herat. I, as a journalist and a member of the group, also went with them to Herat. [. . .] I was about*

Critical moment:
Outbreak of violence

Environment:
Politics, religion
and ethnicity

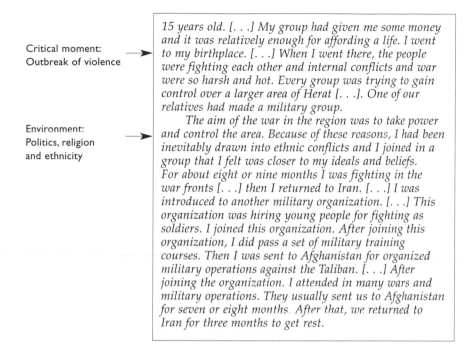

15 years old. [. . .] My group had given me some money and it was relatively enough for affording a life. I went to my birthplace. [. . .] When I went there, the people were fighting each other and internal conflicts and war were so harsh and hot. Every group was trying to gain control over a larger area of Herat [. . .]. One of our relatives had made a military group.

The aim of the war in the region was to take power and control the area. Because of these reasons, I had been inevitably drawn into ethnic conflicts and I joined in a group that I felt was closer to my ideals and beliefs. For about eight or nine months I was fighting in the war fronts [. . .] then I returned to Iran. [. . .] I was introduced to another military organization. [. . .] This organization was hiring young people for fighting as soldiers. I joined this organization. After joining this organization, I did pass a set of military training courses. Then I was sent to Afghanistan for organized military operations against the Taliban. [. . .] After joining the organization. I attended in many wars and military operations. They usually sent us to Afghanistan for seven or eight months. After that, we returned to Iran for three months to get rest.

Identifying Risk Factors and Their Linkages

It is clear from Javad's experience and from all those presented in the foregoing chapters that there are many different factors that result in adolescents joining armed forces or armed groups, and that the relationship between them is neither direct, simple, nor static.

At the same time, what emerges is that there are key factors without which involvement is extremely unlikely, and that these are cumulative as well as interrelated in complex direct and indirect ways. Michael Wessells,[1] looking at children in sub-Saharan Africa of all ages and both volunteers and forced recruits, came to a similar conclusion and developed a preliminary ecological framework[2] comprising: poverty, oppression, ideology, armed conflict, and militarization as macrosocial risk factors, and family, school, and community as microsocial risk factors. The results of the current research refine and vary this suggested framework, while supporting the general approach. In part, the variations reflect the more specific focus on adolescents by bringing out such issues as employment and the links between education and employment. At the same time, our research strongly suggests that the macro- and microsocial factors are fundamentally the same, but that they operate at different levels and with greater specificity as one moves from the general risk level and approaches the point of actual decision. This may represent merely a different classification process rather than any fundamental difference with Wessells's findings.

In the context of adolescents who were not abducted or physically coerced into fighting, the most significant factors identified relate to war, family, poverty, education, and employment. Even as environmental factors, these obviously interrelate. Thus, for example, war often leads to the death or dispersal of family, closure of schools, impoverishment, and lack of employment. Family death or dispersal often leads to impoverishment, the inability of adolescent children to continue in education because of the need to look after younger siblings or to find a means of livelihood for themselves, and, in conflict situations, to their weighing up the benefits of becoming involved.

Since the focus of this research is on involvement in armed forces or armed groups, war itself is the most significant factor. However, as already indicated, the existence of war does not explain why adolescents get involved. The converse is also true. Where peacetime recruitment of adolescents is permitted, the absence of war does not of itself mean that young people will not become involved in armed forces. Indeed, the same key factors appear to be significant in relation to peacetime recruitment as to involvement in armed conflict. The major difference is that war has a "multiplier effect" because it generates so many of the other factors in critical and extreme ways, and also presents what is perceived by the young people as a ready-made solution.

Next to war itself, the family is the most critical factor, whether in pushing or pulling adolescents into armed forces or armed groups. Sometimes this is deliberate: the military family sees the military as a good option, or simply as the natural step. Adolescents often take on responsibility for the family, or the remaining members of it, and the need to provide for their survival, support, and protection. What comes to the fore in the research and has not hitherto been sufficiently appreciated is how often adolescents are in fact seeking to escape from a family situation that appears to them to be abusive, exploitative, humiliating, or in other ways unsatisfactory. Being adolescent, they may well themselves contribute to some of the family problems, as well as being independent enough to seek their own solutions.

For adolescents, the third crucial element is education and employment (or the means of economic livelihood), including the relationship between them. The young person who is in an educational setting and making satisfactory progress, with the prospect of being able to make a living afterwards, or who has already left school and is economically self-sufficient, will require strong incentives to leave to join the armed forces or an armed group. Clearly, this implies various other linkages: the existence and availability of school in practice; a family environment that enables the young person to attend and benefit from school; a school situation that does not diminish, denigrate, humiliate, or discriminate against the young person, and that is relevant to future job prospects. The latter in turn implies the existence of a healthy economic environment with demands for skilled labor and/or opportunities and a market for entrepreneurial skills. At the same time, schools can be recruiting grounds, both directly by armed forces or armed groups, and indirectly by encouraging involvement in the name of religion, ethnicity, nationality, or other ideas.

There are additional factors, such as culture, tradition, role models, and the peer group, but these appear to be less significant in their own right than elements that come into play through the school and the family, or once other factors have already created a vulnerability. Thus, for example, the boy who is already disillusioned with school and in trouble at home is more likely to be influenced by religious or political appeals, or by the decision of friends to join up. Susan Shepler[3] tellingly quotes in this regard from a Sierra Leonean student living in Ghana: "When all our youths are engaged in meaningful activities they won't just follow any so-called freedom fighters who say they are going to liberate them."[4]

What becomes clear from this analysis is that there are major factors of significance to be considered if the phenomenon of adolescent participation in armed forces and armed groups is to be addressed. It is remarkable that in the widely different situations included in this research—geographically, politically, religiously, culturally, and in terms of the conflicts or absence thereof—these major factors emerge as common features. It is interesting to note that most of the same factors were identified by Lars Mjøset and Stephen van Holde as being frequent motives of volunteers in the European armies participating in the Thirty Years War (1618–1648).[5] They specifically list: "deteriorating living conditions (poor people striving to escape starvation, unemployment, tax-pressure, and/or harassment by soldiers); adventurism, religious motives; and the choice of the army as a professional career (clans, bands, families, military dynasties)." In this case, the focus was general rather than specifically on those identified then or now as "children" (that is, under the age of 18), and it is not surprising, therefore, that some of the more "child-specific" elements such as education and family quarrels or abuse do not arise. However, it may be helpful (especially in demythologizing the issue of child soldiers) to recognize that the current problems do have a historical context, and can be considered as a progressive (or regressive) development rather than something entirely new.

Conclusion

At the same time as understanding the risk features common to the situations studied, it is essential to recognize that the degree, weight, and nature of the impact of the risk factors vary in the different situations. Thus, although the major factors identified here provide a useful framework of issues that should always be considered in planning country-specific policies and programs, both the particular aspects of these and the significance of other features will need to be taken into account. For example, in one country it will be the lack of access to any education that is the biggest issue, whereas in another, it will be the content of the education; it may of course be more specific, e.g., there may be particular groups who are excluded from education, or the education may not be seen as relevant. Erika Páez, for example, indicates that girls in Colombia view access to education as a major alternative to joining armed groups, whereas the boys do not see education as a force that can change their lives.[6] By contrast, boys in Sierra Leone rate education as the key to everything,[7] while girls, at least after involvement with the armed groups, cite skills training and economic opportunities more often than formal education as the most important thing for them.[8] Each of the risk factors identified will need to be analyzed and applied in a similar way: Is it all children/young people or particular groups—rural or urban, girls or boys, certain ethnic, religious or linguistic groups, children from single-parent families or living outside the family? Furthermore, there may be additional factors that need to be taken into account in the particular context. What appears to hold true, however, is that even though there are probably more factors, the key areas identified nonetheless remain key areas and will need to be considered in all situations and in relation to all groups of young people.

It is equally clear that each young person is an individual. Even those who share common characteristics with respect to the key issues identified will not all become involved. As the stories of the young people demonstrate, there are many additional and complex factors that may or may not crystallize into a critical moment of decision. They also demonstrate that these young people may be obstreperous, impulsive, and unaware of the full implications of their actions, but that faced with difficult or unbearable circumstances, they do exercise choices, and often display qualities of extraordinary responsibility, courage, persistence, independence, determination, and resilience. Both the individual nature of the circumstances that lead them to take the path they do, and the capacity and personality they demonstrate, require that they should also have a say in planning their future when it comes to demobilization and reintegration.

The results of this research project raise two further issues. First, the question of whether there are differences between girls and boys in their reasons for becoming involved, and what these might mean in terms of planning for demobilization and reintegration. This subject will be considered in the next chapter.

Second, the experiences described here challenge the distinction between "forced" and "voluntary" recruitment. Although all the young people interviewed described themselves as volunteers, the interviews raise a number of questions. Wessells found similar problems: "In many cases, it is unwise to accept so-called voluntary recruitment as a matter of free, rational choice."[9] On the other hand, the fact that young people identify themselves as having volunteered can be presumed to have some significance. This issue is explored further in Chapter 6, both as a practical issue and in relation to the distinction made between forced/compulsory recruitment and volunteers in international legal standards, while recognizing that legal standards are only one facet of a multidimensional problem. A further question that arose from the interviews concerns what it was that the young people thought they were volunteering for; this is also considered.

Notes

1. Wessells 2002, pp. 249–252.
2. Wessells (2002) explains that "ecological approaches to child development feature children's interactions with various actors in the nested social system such as family, community, ethnic gourps, and society. The term 'ecological' underlines the importance of the social context" (pp. 247–248).
3. Shepler, forthcoming.
4. Letter to BBC Focus on Africa, 14 November 2001.
5. Mjøset and van Holde 2002, p. 16.
6. Páez 2001, p. 20.
7. Peters and Richards 1998, pp. 183–210.
8. Bennett 2002.
9. Wessells 2002, p. 247.

5

Girls and Boys

There were more [girls] than what people say. ▪ Vanessa, girl, DRC

We were dangerous! . . . You know that I was with Vanessa in the front line, people had better not come to bother us . . . or we killed you! When you are a girl you have to be harder, or the men they don't respect you. ▪ Christine, girl, DRC

In the course of this research, 53 young soldiers were interviewed, of whom 46 were boys and 7 were girls. Because the size of the sample is so small, this chapter incorporates data from an earlier research project[1] using a similar methodology of in-depth interviews but focused exclusively on adolescent girl soldiers, for which 24 girls were interviewed from four situations,[2] and also takes account of other research.[3] Nevertheless, the findings can only be considered as preliminary, and in many cases raise as many questions as they answer.[4]

As with young soldiers in general, although most attention has been given to the problem of girls who have been abducted, significant numbers of girls in many situations in fact volunteer. Some girls volunteer even in situations where many girls are abducted, such as Sierra Leone and Sri Lanka. Because so little in-depth research has been done, there is insufficient evidence to tell how many girls volunteer in such circumstances. Furthermore, girls in these situations *may* consider it to be in their own interest (retrospectively) to let it be assumed that they, like the majority, were abducted.

In all situations where child soldiers are involved, there are more boys than girls. The proportions vary, but no reports indicate situations where more than one-third of child soldiers are girls.[5] In some situations, there are few reports of participation by girls.[6] But even in such situations, interviews like those reported here throw up indications that girls may be involved indirectly or covertly.[7] One of the boys from Northern Ireland mentioned having seen one or two girls:

> *Um, a few months ago, back, down in the middle of Woodburn, and there was a girl out with a machine gun and the miniskirt and the green top on and the balaclava. And up the Shankill I seen one as well, a girl with a miniskirt and a balaclava. [. . .] And a big massive gun.* ▪ Billy, boy, *Northern Ireland*

Ehtesham, one of the boys from Pakistan, referred to "young ladies" acting as spies in Afghanistan, and of girls being employed by the Taliban to collect strategic information, while Muhammad, also from Pakistan, reported an incident of a "young lady" dropping a bomb from the roof of a house. These may, however, be the exceptions rather than being indications of a larger hidden population of girl participants.

On the other hand, there is, or has been, large-scale involvement of girls in Sri Lanka, Colombia, Sierra Leone,[8] and the Philippines.[9] In both Congo-Brazzaville (a figure of 350 was given by one interviewee) and the Democratic Republic of Congo there were the exclusively female units, the "Amazons," and some of these have continued in the respective armies. Girls were also involved in the liberation struggles in both East Timor[10] and South Africa. The United Kingdom armed forces recruit girls as well as boys.

What does this tell us about the different societies and cultures, or the different nature of the conflicts? At one extreme, the boys in Northern Ireland reacted strongly against the idea that girls could have a role. They saw no role for their wives, sisters, or daughters, and were more likely to say: "This is a man's thing":

> *Because I don't think it's necessary for a girl to be involved. It's up to the men to do what has to be done.* ▪ David, boy, *Northern Ireland*

By contrast, the more underground part of the liberation struggle in East Timor had heavy involvement of girls and women:

> *There were more women than there were men. This was because when we called men to join us they were afraid so that's why we had more women than men. When Indonesians were here, the males were very afraid as they were targeted, and sometimes their parents did not allow them to become involved in politics.* ▪ Helena, girl, *East Timor*

An ILO study of child soldiers in the Philippines suggests a reason for this gender divide: "One explanation is the cultural value placed on the welfare of girls, . . . girls are socialized early in life to undertake domestic chores and other nurturing tasks rather than given instructions of the defense of the homeland or the community. This is considered . . . to be the domain of the males in the family or the community."[11]

This explanation ties in with the findings reported below that girls rarely if ever give religion or ethnicity as their reason for volunteering, but most frequently cite escape from domestic exploitation and abuse. It is also reflected in the disproportionate use of girl soldiers as nurses and medics. The same ILO study discovered that not only were all the girl soldiers assigned to medical teams or food preparation, but no boy soldiers were assigned to medical teams, while an equal number (though not an equal proportion, since only 20 percent of the sample were girls) of boys and girls were assigned to food preparation. The authors observe, "This is a reinforcement of the predominant 'macho-oriented' culture which limits girls' domain of tasks and responsibilities."[12] This may be part of a broader picture associated with the role of the girls in many armed groups being more in the form of auxiliaries than as frontline combatants. However, this is certainly not always the case.

This chapter tries for the first time to compare and contrast the reasons why girls volunteer with why boys do so, starting with the situations where the differences seem strongest.

Religion and Ethnicity

Neither religion nor ethnicity was given as a reason for joining by any of the girls in the interviews. Is this because the girls do not see these as reasons to become involved or because of the greater expectation that boys (males) will fight, but not that girls will? Girls articulated their involvement in the struggle against apartheid in South Africa and against the Indonesian occupation in East Timor[13] in terms of the independence of their countries. In neither case was it stated in terms of one group and its identity but of liberation of the country: Is this a reflection of the nature of the conflict, the way the struggle was portrayed by the leaders, or the way in which the girls themselves conceived of it?

> *Many women joined the clandestine movement because they were searching for the right way to help their country and to get independence.* ▪ Helena, girl, *East Timor*

More what you did at that time, you did it for the community and things like that. [. . .] You did more out of yourself and you did it for the community in which you are living, and for the country, for those who were taken away, and things like that.

▪ Kathryn, girl, South Africa

Domestic Exploitation and Abuse

Both boys and girls give violence at home—for example beatings by a drunken parent—as a reason for joining up:

When my mom arrived, she gave me a beating, wow, she beat me, it was a shame. I mean, she hit me really hard; I mean she treated me really badly. And that was when I, I started seeing those people more. I met some friends there, I used to talk to them, and so they asked me to join the guerrillas.

▪ Carolina, girl, Colombia

However, girls have the additional problem of sexual violence (which none of the boys gave as a reason):

Home life was difficult. My father [stepfather, in fact] was a heavy drinker, he didn't work. He drank and then he struck us all. [Silence] Mom often went to the fields, she left us with him, and he drank and struck us. [Silence] When he drank a lot, he did as if I was his wife. [. . .] I left because he beat us, he drank, and then he took me as his wife. I preferred to die in the war rather than to stay at home and to keep on suffering. ▪ Vanessa, girl, *DRC*

In addition, girls are often treated as domestic servants within their own family, or in their extended family:

When I was older, the wife kept me home and didn't allow me to go to school. I had to work at home. I did all the work at home from cooking to cleaning, washing, and everything I could possibly do, and what I could not do was forced on me. ▪ Abarimi, girl, *Sri Lanka*[14]

Some of the young people recognized that their own behavior was a factor in the way they were treated at home:

I made them get angry. I mean, I was quite bad at home, and so they used to beat me quite a lot, and I didn't like it that they beat me for what I did, but they were right to beat me for doing that.

■ Alfredo, boy, *Colombia*

What is different is the very high incidence of domestic violence and exploitation as the sole or main reason for joining given by *girls*: other reasons were the exception rather than the rule. Despite the small sample, common sense suggests that this finding may be accurate: in many societies girls are confined to the domestic scene more than boys and therefore not only are they more vulnerable to abuse or exploitation there but they also have fewer avenues for escape. Erika Páez estimates that in Colombia some 40 percent of the girls who join the armed groups do so because of family abuse and domestic violence.[15] She also points out that, "although boys also experience domestic violence, the difference is that, as workers in the field, they have more independence. This makes the pressure of abuse less intense."[16] Although this is undoubtedly true, it must not be forgotten how many of the boys interviewed for this research—particularly from Colombia and Sri Lanka—also gave domestic violence as a reason for volunteering.[17]

Girls also articulate a specific frustration about not being listened to—not having a real say in deciding their own future, particularly in relation to marriage, but also more generally:

That's what I hated about my family, they never would've listened to whatever reason I told them. ■ Sonia, girl, *Philippines*

I wanted to get away from the marriage my parents were planning to force me into. I really got disturbed, they were forcing me. [. . .] About ten days before the marriage, I started to plan to leave the house. I waited, tried to convince my parents, they were very adamant and would not listen to me. I tried to inform them about my wishes through my good friend and even through a relative. They never listened. The day before the marriage everything was ready. I ran away. ■ Punitha, girl, *Sri Lanka*[18]

This reinforces the sense that these girls are ones who possess strength, independence, courage, persistence, and character. They are seeking a life of their own and behaving in ways that are contrary to societal expectations as well as against the wishes of their family.

The question of violence within the family reported in these cases needs to be put in the context of how few of these young people were living in a stable family situation. According to the information they provided at the time when they joined the armed forces or armed group, only 20 of the 53 interviewees were living at home with both natural parents. The reasons for this were sometimes directly related to the war, such as killing or displacement, and sometimes not—death from natural causes, separation, divorce, or suicide.

None of the sexual abuse recorded in these (few) cases was actually incestuous. It all occurred either where there was a stepfather or where the girl was sent to her extended family. Often a difficult girl was sent to extended family, where she became the subject of unwanted sexual attention from, for example, the older sister's husband. Sometimes the physical abuse arose in the context of the mother's fear of the daughter becoming sexually involved with the stepfather. Sometimes physical abuse occurred where there was also sexual abuse—either by the abusive stepparent, or by the mother, or by siblings, and not necessarily linked in any way to sexual abuse. In such instances, the mother was often physically abused by the new partner too. Sonia's stepfather only stopped beating her mother when Sonia (girl, the Philippines) joined the New People's Army (NPA) and threatened to come back and kill him if he continued.

Both girls and boys reported physical abuse or humiliation at the hands of either stepparents and/or natural parents. Since this research focused on the adolescent age group, this is perhaps not surprising and such behavior did not necessarily betoken a lack of love of the parent for the child. For teenagers to run away from home is not uncommon. The difference for these teenagers is the irrevocability of the decision (in most instances) and the short- and long-term effects.

Alfredo (boy, Colombia) was beaten at home, but recognized that this was sometimes due to his own bad behavior:

My dad, well, I've realized now that what he was doing for me was actually right, he was helping me. I had to be a serious person. I shouldn't be alone, or doing bad things, but doing what was right, working, always trying to make a success out of my life, but I didn't pay any attention to him. [. . .] I always did the opposite of what my dad said, and so that's why what happened to me is what happened to me.

Alfredo was attracted by the guerrillas and their guns, and joined them when he was 14, on an occasion when his father was angry with him.

His father did not know, but suspected and went looking for him, but could not find him. Eventually, one of Alfredo's comrades in the guerrillas told his father, who tried to persuade the guerrillas to let Alfredo return, but they would not because by then he had seen the camp and knew where they were. Clearly the father loved Alfredo—he had gone to get him back before—when Alfredo had run away to an uncle when he was 10:

> *Well, the memory I have is when I was at home with my mom and my dad. Now I miss them a lot, and that's the memory I always think of. I mean, I'd really like to be with them all the time now, but it's too late now.*

Alfredo missed his father and so he ran away from the guerrillas, but he was recaptured and punished. While serving his punishment he again planned to run away. The second time he succeeded in escaping and gave himself up to the army.

Societal Expectations and Roles

Some girls joined in order to assert their equality with boys:

> *You know, I come from a warrior's family; as far as I remember, my father has always been in the rebellion; [. . .] I always wanted to be with my father, to listen to the stories, the plans; and then my brothers, they were with him also. [. . .] In fact, it's because I was a girl. I was the only girl with three brothers, I wanted to help the rebellion, I thought that if my brothers could do it, well so could I. I wanted to do like my brothers. When you are little, you want to do as if you were tall, when you are a girl, do as if you were a boy.*
>   ▪ Catherine, girl, *DRC*

The assertion of equality may be not only in the act of joining, but in the social structure within the group itself. This is a feature that many of the girls in the NPA (Philippines) appreciated:

> *A woman can do what a man can. We were all equal.*
>   ▪ Sonia, girl, *Philippines*

In dramatic contrast, where societal expectations and roles played a part in the boys' decision to volunteer, it was in conforming to rather than rebelling against these preconceptions, submitting to peer group and community pressure, and accepting the image of boys as fighters:

One good reason [for joining] was that I have spent time in Pakistan [Punjab] and people used to call us pulse-eaters[19] and [so I wanted] to escape the ostracism that I was afraid of fighting. [. . .] My father had a reputation and my refusal might not bring good fame for him.
■ Muhammad, boy, *Pakistan*

Family expectations also have their part to play. Both boys and girls who came from a family who had "always" been involved in a military group gave this as a factor in their involvement. For the boys, it was expected of them, and/or they expected it of themselves. It was not expected of Catherine, the girl in the DRC, but because she was the only girl in a family with a father and brothers involved, she wanted to participate as well. She also saw it as an issue of equality between herself and her brothers: Why should she be excluded from this part of the family tradition?

Jessica (girl, Colombia) joined out of love for her brother who was already in the FARC, although she had other brothers (stepbrothers?) and uncles who were in the paramilitaries. It was her brother's involvement—and, more specifically, his coming to fetch her—that triggered her joining up; equally, it was her brother's decision to leave that led to her own (reluctant) departure from the FARC too.

Many boys, but not the girls, spoke of the attraction of the military in general or of the fictional images presented by Rambo-style films, or of international, national, or local individual soldiers or militants as real-life role models.[20]

We were inspired by the films; war films, spy films. [. . .] you believe that it's reality, that it's easy. ■ Pascal, boy, *Congo-Brazzaville*

One particular person who was influential in this thing, it was the whole idea of Che Guevara being an international fighter. [. . .] What we talked about was that he played such a role that the world actually—even we—could do things that way. [. . .] Indirectly, I can say that this is what actually influenced one.
■ Samuel, boy, *South Africa*

When you feel the heat in a neighborhood, when you begin to fire shots around, you start to smoke marijuana, you're almost the tough guy of the neighborhood. Then people see, this guy's like that, not a— you see? Many, many things, he's the one who kills most, he's got the

most heads under his belt, you understand? The one who's got the
most deaths notched up, most "jobs" because—you see, the one who's
robbed most, stolen the most cars, motorbikes, automobiles.
▪ Carlos, boy, *Colombia*

"Simply the Best" is the one [song] for the UFF [Ulster Freedom
Fighters] because they are. [. . .] If I was asked, I dunno. I would
think about it, I'd like to be. Everyone would like to be. [. . .] Well,
I don't know, 'cause you're up there, the highest, you can't get nay
higher. ▪ Billy, boy, *Northern Ireland*

The "Do's" [formal or semiformal social event] and people would
come out with guns and all and you'd say, "I want to be one of
them." ▪ Paul, boy, *Northern Ireland*

It may be the pull of these military images that added to the attraction
of guns for the boys:

You got like a buzz when you done it, like I don't know, all the
adrenalin and all. Like when you pick the gun up.
▪ Billy, boy, *Northern Ireland*

This fascination with guns was rare among the girls. Some recognized
that being issued a gun by the armed group was an acknowledgment of
their status as full members. Some saw the gun as their means of protection. Few speak of the actual attraction of weapons per se, although
one of the girls did:

Because all my life I've liked guns. . . . Because I was brought up by
my family and they also like guns. ▪ Jessica, girl, *Colombia*

Protection for Self and Family

Meeting societal and family expectations in a more positive fashion, it
was again the boys and not the girls who felt pressure to provide for, and
especially to feed, their families. This, of course, is strongest for the eld-
est or only son in the family, which may be one of the factors explaining why some but not all (male) children of the same family join:

That is when I tried, since my sister was pregnant. There was no one
to look after her. That is why I took up arms. [. . .] I participated a

Girls are also involved in active combat

Photo by T. Voeten

little in the offensive, once we recaptured some ground, we were authorized to loot in the homes. I was now able to provide for my family. There you are, that is what made me stay in the army.

▪ Albert, boy, *Congo-Brazzaville*

Both girls and boys were acutely aware of issues of ill treatment of civilians, both in general and specifically. For girls, their particular vulnerability to abuse—rape, abduction, and so on—was a trigger factor to protect themselves by taking up arms. For boys, the need to protect female members of their family from sexual abuse was a factor:

When you are a girl, you know what men will do; you will be abused, you catch diseases, you can have children, you must pay great attention. [. . .] You must be wary of the boys, the men here, they believe that they can treat you how they want, they don't ask whether you agree or not. ▪ Christine, girl, *DRC*

When there is the war and you are a woman, you risk your life; you risk your life because you are a woman and the men will rape you if you don't protect yourself. When they go in the villages, they will catch the small girls, the mothers, even the grandmothers, and they abuse them. Then they take you along with them and they still rape you or they kill you then. There are many girls who have children but who didn't decide. [. . .] Then when you know what the men do, you will make the war with them, like that, you have a weapon and you can protect yourself. ▪ Vanessa, girl, *DRC*

I signed up to protect my sisters, because a lot of boys attacked girls, women, and mothers. [. . .] I had to pay [. . .] to stop the militaries from taking my sister. ▪ Albert, boy, *Congo-Brazzaville*

Both boys and girls reacted against their experience of armed forces or groups killing, torturing, or ill-treating members of their family:

I hate the Indonesian military because of what my mother told me they had done to her in the past. [. . .] After I had my Confirmation ceremony at the Catholic Church, we were celebrating and the TNI [Indonesian military] and Brimob [riot police] came to our house and destroyed parts of the house and arrested one of my brothers. Those things made me very irritated. [. . .] At that time I felt very afraid but after they had left I felt very angry and kept this feeling in my heart.

▪ Helena, girl, *East Timor*

My father and brother were taken away and they came and shot my mother and little sister. I loved them so much. My family, a nice happy family, was destroyed. With my bare hands, crying so much, my sister and I dug the grave for my mother and sister. We were just small children. Now I can tell you that I grew up overnight. I became like a big person and I took the decision to join the LTTE. I was very angry and wanted to take revenge. ▪ Sayanathen, boy, *Sri Lanka*

In this context, it is noticeable that the "Amazons" expressed no regret for killing soldiers (including their own) who, despite their efforts to prevent them, committed rape. For them, this was an issue of "self-protection."

Education

Interestingly, education and access to it did not seem to occur as a major factor for girls in their decision to join. This may reflect the fact that for many of them, lack of access to education is the norm rather than the exception. That said, one girl from Sri Lanka in fact ran away because she could not cope with the pressure to succeed at school:

My parents had very high hopes regarding my future. I was afraid that I would let them down because I knew that I was not a clever student. I was struggling to satisfy them because I loved them. During my school days all the time I had to go for tuition, I had no free time to have a hobby. . . . Before the exam—I knew I would never be able to fulfill their desire, so I had plans to leave and run away. I ran away because I found it difficult to study. I didn't want to make them sad and hurt by failing my exam. . . . Running away from home was not easy, but to escape facing the examination I knew that I would fail made me take this hard decision.
▪ Kavitha, girl, *Sri Lanka*[21]

However, it is interesting to note that in Colombia, Páez gives access to education as apparently being seen by girls as a major alternative to joining the armed groups, but not by boys.[22] It is possible that these findings are not in fact mutually contradictory. Girls who were being exploited or abused domestically were unlikely to be receiving education, but it was the former that was the major reason for them joining. However, given the choice of getting an education or joining an armed group, they would state their preference for education. Furthermore, this could also be linked to an assumption that attending school or college would not mean staying in or returning to an abusive situation, but either being in a better family situation or having independence.

Reaction to Involvement

Some girls bitterly regret their decision to join, feeling that perhaps after all life at home was not so bad:

Well, now that I've been through that experience, the truth is that was a disaster for me. ▪ Carolina, girl, *Colombia*

Now I realize that it is worse than failing an exam.
▪ Kavitha, girl, *Sri Lanka*

I ran away to escape a marriage I didn't like. I ended up in a worse setup now and that's what I have earned. ▪ Punitha, girl, *Sri Lanka*

For these girls, this can result in them having trouble taking decisions since they feel that the important decision they made turned out to be so wrong.[23] This suggests that these girls take personal responsibility for their actions and decisions.

Susan Shepler[24] identifies a difference in the "discourse" available to girls and boys in Sierra Leone. Whereas the latter seek—and are permitted—to absolve themselves from blame by abdicating responsibility on the basis that they were forced, drugged, had no other choice, and so on, girls do not attempt to do so even though their circumstances were very similar. She concludes that in Sierra Leone it is easier for a boy to be accepted after amputating the hands of villagers, than for a girl to be accepted after being the victim of rape. It is not clear whether this is universally true, or relates to specific situations or circumstances: the link to actual or perceived sexual activity may be one of the keys. For example, UNICEF reports that in El Salvador "girls have not reported being stigmatized by their family or community for having sexual relations and children outside marriage,"[25] although the problem of their needs not being taken into account in planning programs still existed. Care, therefore, needs to be taken in making generalizations about the particular problems and social attitudes.

On the other hand some girls feel that they gained from the experience:

*From my experience in the clandestine movement I learned about
moral courage, discipline, how to organize ourselves, and also how to
explain the movement to other friends. [. . .] All the work I have done
was interesting and even now I want to continue to help people.*
▪ Helena, girl, *East Timor*

Many of the girls are, and admit to being, affected by the deaths of
comrades as well as by deaths they inflicted. More, though not all, of
the boys tend to take such things for granted: Is this an actual difference, or an assumed one because of societal expectations? Many boys
as well as girls objected to the torture, ill-treatment, and arbitrary
killings they saw, and they sought to avoid participating in such acts,
and in some cases this was a key factor in their decision to leave again.
Some of the girls went further:

*We tried to prevent [the boys from committing rapes] but if they are
doped it's difficult, so sometimes you must kill them. If you can't kill
them at this time, well you kill them when you are on the front line.*
▪ Vanessa, girl, *DRC*

In some armed opposition movements—certainly the NPA[26] in the
Philippines and the FARC in Colombia—girls are expected to provide
the medical services. This does not mean that girls are not also active
combatants. This is not a new development but reflects the experience
of women in, for example, the Yugoslav national liberation struggle in
1941–1945.[27]

Demobilization and Reintegration

Girls, even those who were beaten by their mothers and who ran away
from home because of physical abuse and the feeling that they were
never listened to, miss their mothers and want to be reconciled with
them:

*I wanted to study and work for a better life for my mother and I.
I know that she sacrificed a lot since the day I was born.*
▪ Sonia, girl, *Philippines*

For many girls this is part of a broader pattern. Yvonne Keairns
concludes: "The girls are not searching for ways to retaliate and bring

harm to those who had used and misused them. They were looking for ways to make a contribution, to do something meaningful and productive with their life and to make up for the harm they have delivered upon others."[28]

However, for some girls as well as boys, enrollment in the army (once they were of age) seemed the only viable future:

> *When there was the demobilization, some were already adults, so they went to the army. Almost all the soldiers are former child soldiers. The army, it's the only job here, so you stay in the army to stay alive.*
> ▪ Vanessa, girl, *DRC*

Particular problems arise for girls on demobilization and reintegration and/or at the end of the conflict.[29] For a start, many girls do not make it into the demobilization process at all.[30] Because there are no accurate (or even approximately accurate) figures of the number of child soldiers in any situation, let alone a good breakdown between boys and girls, all figures will be indicative, but for example, in Sierra Leone it has been reported that 8 percent of demobilized soldiers were female,[31] with only 3 percent of demobilized child soldiers being girls in the "most recent phase" (as of 2002).[32] By contrast, 11 percent of demobilized ex-soldiers in El Salvador were female.[33]

There are many different reasons why girls do not go through the formal demobilization. Sometimes the role of girls as "soldiers," as opposed to camp followers, wives, or concubines, is not recognized by those planning and organizing the demobilization process, and so they are screened out.[34] Sometimes girls are reluctant to identify themselves as having been involved because of the negative repercussions in terms of reintegration and possible prospects, including marriage, where this is viewed in negative terms. It has been suggested that sometimes male soldiers and commanders may wish to "hold on to" the girls to compensate for their loss of power in themselves being demobilized, or because the girls are more useful than boys once the fighting stops, continuing to undertake household and family tasks.[35] An example of the multiple discrimination that ensues if girls are excluded (by themselves or others) from going through the formal demobilization process, arises in relation to what otherwise seems an excellent scheme: in Sierra Leone, not only were school fees waived for demobilized child soldiers who had a demobilization number, but also schools accepting them received a package of materials usable for all their students to encourage inclusion of former child soldiers. Girl soldiers who did not formally demobilize, therefore, neither received the school fee waiver, nor brought benefits to the school.[36]

Many of the girls have babies. Some of them are still in a relationship with the father who is trying to support them, but when he too is or was a child soldier, this compounds the difficult transition to economic viability. Some are rejected by the "husband"[37]:

> *The last time when I asked him if that's the way to treat me, he only told me that now the war is over; we only got married while the war lasted—now that the war has ended the marriage should be ended too.*
> ▪ Elisabeth, girl, *Sierra Leone*

Others do not know where the "husband" is, or he is dead. This makes their access to education, vocational training, and employment even more difficult, both in terms of looking after the baby, and also because they need to support themselves and the baby financially during this time. In addition, in many societies, the economic activities open to girls are in any case more limited than for boys. This is compounded by their involvement in the conflict, and the "evidence" of the baby may stigmatize them because of the implications of sexual activity. Rehabilitation programs need to be adapted to take account of the specific needs of girl soldiers, and of girl soldiers with babies, taking into account the sociocultural context.[38] Such provision needs to be flexible enough so that where the girl is in a relationship with the father of her baby, he can be accommodated and brought into the program as well. While the girls in the DRC took up arms to protect themselves, Elisabeth (Sierra Leone) recognized that the first step in protection there was to surrender herself to a "commander" so that she was taken as his "wife" rather than being raped. In this way, she joined the RUF and then was taught the use of arms, fought, and in the course of time was promoted to lieutenant. Some of the girls, as well as many of the boys, acquire drinking and drug habits while in the armed forces or an armed group.

For both girls and boys, the relationship with the family is unlikely to have improved during their absence. Since many were running away from home in the first place, the question of how to reestablish connections with the family may be more complex than for those children who were recruited by force.

Conclusion

Although many of the same factors drive or lead girls and boys to join armed forces and armed groups, there are also differences and variations in the degree or emphasis of the separate factors. These differences reflect the status and role of girls in the society from which they come. For girls, participation in the conflict tends to exacerbate this problem, because their participation is usually countercultural and is often associated, rightly or wrongly, with perceptions of them being sexually active.[39] This is not a new problem; Gretchen Ritter[40] documents both legal and societal discrimination against U.S. female veterans after World War II: "Employers were not inclined to believe that women learned anything useful in the services, and may have had questions about the moral standing of women veterans given the slander campaigns of previous years."[41]

The experience of Angola, Mozambique, and Zimbabwe in using traditional methods of cleansing the child soldiers in order to make the break between their violent (military) life and their social reintegration and future, is worth taking into account. Cleansing rituals are used to wash away the evil spirits of the murdered, which are believed to hang around the soldier who killed them and can bring sickness, infertility, and misfortune to the family. Without this cleansing, an ex-combatant may not be accepted back into his or her community. Although the accounts of Irma Aarsman and Alcinda Honwana[42] only give instances in relation to boys, Carol Thompson[43] cites the case of an abducted girl. This still leaves open the question of girls who were not abducted, and also whether they would want to be "reintegrated" into a situation and societal role from which they had sought to escape. These broader issues, in addition to the specific factors identified, need to be addressed both in order to reduce the incidence of girls joining up, and in order to provide them with effective socioeconomic reintegration after demobilization.

Both girls and boys prioritize education and skills training in order to be able to engage in a viable economic activity at reintegration. For the girls, difficulties are compounded by societal attitudes, and by the more limited economic activities generally available to them in any case. Where they have babies, there is the added problem of ensuring that they have access to education and vocational training opportunities and the need for practical arrangements, such that access in principle translates into real access.[44]

Where HIV/AIDS and/or other sexually transmitted diseases are prevalent, the need for both girls and boys to have education about and access to appropriate health provision is obvious. Girls may face the additional health and psychological problems associated with forced sexual activity, and childbirth or abortion. The need to ensure that they are not discriminated against by exclusion, deliberate or accidental, from demobilization and reintegration processes, must be balanced by the need for girls to be able to access education, skills training, health services, and so on without having to identify themselves as having been involved with the armed forces or armed groups if they choose to conceal this in what they perceive as their best interests.

On the other hand, although sometimes the impact has been over-rated, war has at times been the occasion for societal change in particu-lar in relation to the role of women.[45] Shepler notes some positive trends in Sierra Leone in this respect, with some teenage mothers being accepted back by their families, and even being allowed to return to school.[46]

Notes

1. "The Lived Experience of Girl Child Soldiers," a joint research proj-ect of the Quaker UN Offices in New York and Geneva, with which Rachel Brett was associated, and the use of which has been agreed upon. The results are available in Keairns 2002, 2003a, 2003b, and 2003c.

2. The situations were Angola, Colombia, the Philippines, and Sri Lanka. Thus two of them directly supplemented the interviews for this research. Those for the Philippines brought in an additional situation. Angola is not relevant for this purpose since all the girls interviewed had been abducted.

3. In particular, Cagoco-Guiam 2002; Camacho, Balanon, and Verba 2001; Dumas and de Cock 2003; and UNICEF 2002—the original interviews of the girls from this study were made available courtesy of UNICEF EAPRO.

4. The general neglect of the issue of girl soldiers is documented in McKay and Mazurana 2000. One of the reasons for this neglect is neatly illus-trated by the fact that Peters and Richards's article (1998b), "Why We Fight: Voices of Youth Combatants in Sierra Leone," which refers to girl soldiers and includes an interview with one, has the short title on the subsequent pages "Boy Soldiers in Sierra Leone"!

5. In the ILO Rapid Assessment of Child Soldiers in the Philippines, 20 percent of the respondents were girls. The highest percentage of female com-batants (with no distinction between ages) reported in the International Com-mitte of the Red Cross's *Women and War* study is 30 percent, so the proportion of girl soldiers in relation to boy soldiers reflects the more general gender breakdown in this respect (Lindsay 2001, p. 23).

6. Nordstrom (1997) was one of the first to recognize the absence of com-ment, question, and discussion about the participation of girls in warfare.

7. This is also the conclusion of UNICEF (2002, p. 19) and of Dumas and de Cock (2003, p. 19).

8. Richards (2002, p. 262) gives a figure of 5–10 percent female fighters in the RUF, distinct from the RUF's "combat wives unit" and "combat support unit."

9. Studied in "The Lived Experience of Girl Child Soldiers" research project: Keairns 2002, 2003a, 2003b, and 2003c.

10. UNICEF 2002.

11. Cagoco-Guiam 2002, p. 26.
12. Ibid., pp. 38 and 46.
13. UNICEF 2002, p. 27.
14. Keairns 2003c.
15. Páez, 2001, p. 13.
16. Ibid., p. 14.
17. See in particular Chapters 2 and 3 of this volume.
18. Keairns 2003c.
19. According to the interviewer, this is "a pejorative term used by people in the North West Frontier Province about the people of the Punjab who use a lot of pulses [legumes] in their diet, implying that they are unreliable or cowardly."
20. It is noteworthy that all these military/heroic role models are male.
21. Keairns 2003.
22. Páez 2001, p. 20.
23. Keairns 2002.
24. Shepler 2002.
25. UNICEF 2000, pp. 3–4.
26. This is also the conclusion of Cagoco-Guiam (2002).
27. Jancar 1988.
28. Keairns 2003c.
29. More generally on demobilization and reintegration of child soldiers, see United Nations Department of Peacekeeping Operations, Lessons Learned Unit (2000, pp. 84–92).
30. Less than 2 percent of demobilized children in Liberia in the 1997–1998 exercise were girls (David 1998, p. 20).
31. Sierra Leone National Committee for Disarmament, Demobilization and Reintegration (NCDDR) 2002. Zack-Williams (2001, p. 80) states that "605 of the 1,000 fighters screened by the Disarmament and Resettlement Unit set up by the President before the May 1997 coup were women."
32. United Nations Organization for the Coordination of Humanitarian Affairs (UNOCHA) 2002, p. 47.
33. Spencer 1997.
34. Thompson (1999, p. 202) comments that given that a UNICEF study was completed in 1990 that identified the problem of women and girls "attached" to soldiers as an overlooked issue, "it is quite astonishing that Mozambican girls and women still accompanying soldiers at the time of demobilization in 1994 were not counted, addressed, nor cared for."
35. David 1998, p. 20.
36. Bennett 2002, p. 61.
37. David (1998, p. 21) states that in Liberia, "many high ranking faction officials, for instance, jettisoned the women they 'married' during the war, only to marry more 'respectable' women when it was over."
38. Dumas and de Cock 2003, p. 23.
39. The heavy bias of the research literature on the demobilization and reintegration programs in Liberia, Sierra Leone, Angola, and Mozambique has to be borne in mind when considering other situations. The experiences in other regions—for example, Nicaragua, El Salvador, Colombia, the Philippines, Sri Lanka, and indeed in other African countries such as South Africa, Eritrea, and

Ethiopia—may identify different societal attitudes as being the most problematic for girl soldiers, or find that in some cases this is not an issue.

40. Ritter 2002, p. 222.

41. See also Shepler's (2002) point about the different discourses available to boys and girls in Sierra Leone.

42. Aarsman 1993; Honwana 1999.

43. Thompson 1999.

44. This was recognized as a problem as long ago as 1997, in the review of experience in El Salvador. See Spencer 1997, p. 47.

45. Spencer (1997) gives both positive and negative developments in post-conflict Nicaragua and El Salvador in this respect.

46. Shepler 2002.

6

The Concept of Volunteering

The question of whether the decision to join an armed force or armed group was or was not voluntary arises in two different contexts. The first is practical. If youngsters have chosen to become involved and the circumstances that led to that decision have not changed significantly, they are more likely to return—even if they are demobilized—than those who were abducted or physically forced into military service. The second aspect is the legal one, and concerns the international instruments that apply to the military involvement of young people. Both are examined in this chapter.

Volunteering for What?

Because so little research has been done into the specific reasons why young people join armed forces and armed groups when they are not abducted or physically forced to do so, it tends to be assumed that those who join want to fight. This is true in some cases:

> *Besides religious inclination and spirit, it was my dream to take part in a combat [Jihad] and I got a chance to fulfill my dream. Moreover, it was also my desire to observe people fighting and how they use various kinds of weapons.* • Aziz, Pakistan

However, it is not true in many others. As has been shown in the earlier chapters of this book, there are many different factors and reasons that lead young people to join:

It was not because I wanted to join the movement to fight. I wanted to get away from the marriage my parents were planning to force me into. ▪ Punitha, *Sri Lanka*

Some of these relate to their perceived lack of other choices:

I think unemployment is the main temptation. If you have nothing to get busy with then you want to go and experience something adventurous. When one has no choice then the ultimate result is that he decides: "Why not try and join the combat [Jihad] rather than lying dull?" ▪ Aziz, *Pakistan*

Even when a positive choice is made to join, it is not always with a desire, or even intention, to fight. Initially, membership of the group may not entail a combat role:

First, I was among the supporting forces that provide food and dress for the fighters. Actually, I was a coordinator and organizer to provide food, and provide in particular bread from inside of the city for our soldiers. My duty was to make contact with bakers and butchers and ask them to provide bread and food. [. . .] But in the last year, in 2002, I had to fight, because there was a lack of human force and the Taliban forces entered Mazar. ▪ Hassan, *Afghanistan*

In 1993, I began to work for a military group [. . .] the Hezbollah. Hezbollah had a magazine [. . .]. My job was to gather news and information for that magazine. I must listen to radios and collect news about Afghanistan. I must record all news and transcribe them and edit and provide them for publications. [. . .] I slept in the office of the group at night, because I did not have any place, and on days I worked there for them. [. . .] In 1995 our group moved. I, as a journalist and a member of the group, also went with them.
                                                    ▪ Javad, *Afghanistan*

Andrés (Colombia), the quiet sensitive student who was picked on at his new school, and ended up killing someone and having to move away, joined an armed group because he saw it as both protection for himself and as a protection service to the community. He still says that the thing he likes least is "killing someone, I almost— that feeling lingers with you afterwards, I don't really like taking someone else's life," even though he acknowledges having killed "several" people.

Jessica (Colombia) was particularly haunted by having to kill three of her former companions when she and her brother were escaping from the guerrillas. Similarly:

> *When I think about it—that I might have killed someone—I feel afraid, uneasy and guilty. If I did shoot anybody, I feel sorry for him.*
> ▪ Sonia, *Philippines*

As some of them point out, for many of them deciding whether to join an armed group is a stark choice between eating and not eating:

> *When the rebels invaded the town of Makeni, my parents fled the town and even myself, but without knowing that my parents had left. I was only told by a friend that they had left, but I did not believe it so I went to look for them in the town. When I got into town, I found nobody there again so I had nothing to eat and there was nobody to be responsible for me. So when the rebels came, I decided to go to them so that they could give me food to eat and survive.*
> ▪ Augustine, *Sierra Leone*

Others want only to provide for their families and see no alternative:

> *There are many common points in the stories. For example, one of the boys whom we met [. . .] his mother was old, his sister was sick and she had two little children, the father was not there. And people are there and told you to come, to join; and thought it was a means of having money [. . .] it isn't the desire for going to make the war or whatever, he didn't want to go to do that; he wanted to do something else, but when it's the only opportunity . . .*
> ▪ (*Congo-Brazzaville* interviewer)

Some are looking for a job, and the army is the employer at hand. Or they are looking for education or training and this is what is promised to them. Andrew (United Kingdom) realized he had made a mistake in the college course he had enrolled in:

> *I looked into the army and I got to find out about further education. And the amount of things you can actually do and get trained in, it's*

exactly the same as going to college really. Plus I wouldn't have to wait another year, an added bonus, and I got paid for it.

Some join because they think they want to fight, without knowing the reality of what they are getting into:

When I was younger, I watched a lot of action films; it encouraged me to take up a weapon. [. . .] I joined the rebellion at 10 years old, so you know, the films coupled with dictatorship, is encouraging enough. [. . .] I hung out with a Rwandan major. [. . .] I wanted to learn, to discover, to know what it was; so he motivated me, he influenced me. And you know, him and his soldiers, they were so chic in their uniforms. Above all, my parents travelled a lot—I was left at home with my brothers and sisters. [. . .] My parents were away [. . .] so I would hang out with the major. And one day, the major took me to the training center. ▪ Germain, DRC

Although Germain seems generally bright and "macho," when he talks about the death of children, including some of his friends, in the container in which they were transported to the training center, and other deaths during training, it is clear that these have affected him deeply, and continue to do so. Although he had initially joined "voluntarily," his experience during combat when he was 12 years old raises questions about how "voluntary" the participation of these young people really is:

I was injured by shatters of a projective explosion in Kisangani [he still bears the scars on his foot]. It was very painful. They took me away to be treated, but after two months I was forced back to combat. [. . .] You are told that if you do not wish to progress, in that case you would be shot!

How Voluntary Is Voluntary?

Involuntarily—if you have nothing—you volunteer for the army. Involuntarily, because the situation requires it. ▪ Michel, DRC

I didn't choose this situation. You know that we are in a country at war, and then you don't have much choice. You can run away or fight. ▪ Christine, DRC

All the young soldiers interviewed for this research identified themselves as having volunteered. However, their actual descriptions of why
they joined and the analysis resulting from them raise serious questions
about how many of them could be classified as volunteers objectively,
as well as more generally the question of how "voluntary" is defined.[1]
Arthur (Sierra Leone) identified himself as having volunteered, but he
had also witnessed the murder of his friend who refused to join. Knowing that if you do not join you are likely to be shot is not the way in
which most people conceptualize the idea of voluntary recruitment.

Others may choose to join, but then discover that the reality is not
what they had imagined:

*In the beginning, we enjoyed the adventure of fighting and were
very active, but after a week or two got fed up as some people were
wounded, others were killed, some fell victim to land mines and blew
up. Personally I escaped narrow deaths—once I was riding a tank and
as I jumped down it struck an antitank land mine and it blew into
pieces. Such incidents made us reluctant to go to the front line.*

■ Aziz, Pakistan

*And when I did do the active stuff it was a big culture shock. Like
some of the stuff—when I first went back up [to Northern Ireland—
Stephen had been there as a 17-year-old but not allowed out on the
streets] . . . there were people out there who really wanted to kill you
and you have to keep on your toes.* ■ Stephen, United Kingdom

*When I was younger, I watched a lot of action films; it encouraged
me to take up a weapon. . . . You look at action films; when you look
at that you are impressed! I said to myself, why just him? I said to
myself that one day, it would be me, I could also do that. Learning
how to handle weapons, fighting in the front line, knowing how it
happens. . . . You see, at the beginning I didn't think of that, because
I watched the television, and I didn't know the consequences and how
it could happen, and so on. I didn't think of that, I was still a kid.
I was so impressed by the actions, the way of handling the weapons,
their way of getting dressed. I said to myself that one day, I would
also wear the same outfit. . . . I didn't know that in the army, I
would suffer.* ■ Germain, DRC

Many kids watch and dream. The difference is that most are not in
a situation where the temptation and opportunity to try it out is so readily available. For others, the temptation is compounded by one of the

environmental push factors explored in earlier chapters—abuse or exploitation at home, absence of a home environment, and/or unhappy school experience, or exclusion from school.

Among armed forces and armed groups, it is unusual to permit recruits, even children, to leave again, though some manage to escape. The NPA (the Philippines) is a rare exception in apparently permitting young people to go home if they decide they do not want to join after trying it out:

> *I was still given choice to go home if I felt that life with them was too difficult.* ▪ Sonia, *Philippines*

Some young people are aware, at least at an intellectual level, that they are making a long-term commitment:

> *But when you join, you join for life.* ▪ Billy, *Northern Ireland*

Many, however, do not realize the irrevocable nature of the decision they are taking. This is part of their incomplete understanding of warfare. They discover too late that even if the initial act was voluntary, there is no opportunity to exercise further choice:

> *We endured it, because we were far away from the city, in the bush; furthermore, land mines surrounded us.* ▪ Urbain, *DRC*

> *You know, sometimes, even very often, I would cry when I thought of my family, I even almost committed suicide! At times it is so difficult, I would have died rather than continue like this! Although I had a friend, he helped me a lot. He was there for me when I was depressed. After being seriously injured (for the second time), I recall that there was someone by me all the time, but I thought it was a nurse. But then I realized that it was my mother . . . she paid all the hospital treatment you know. [Silence] I asked for her forgiveness, she began to cry, so did I; she spoke of our family, my father, our family, you know. She wanted to take me back home with her. [. . .] She asked permission, from a superior, to take me home with her; he told her that a soldier could never go back as a civilian and that if I had been hospitalized it was so that I could go back to fight. They took me back. [Silence] She was against it. [Silence] My mother really wanted to take me back, so they transferred me to another hospital without telling her.* ▪ Germain, *DRC*

No, they were not able to escape freely because if you were caught trying to escape you would be killed. . . . one man wanted to escape. He was caught and killed on the spot. . . . They killed him and threw his body into the river. ▪ Elisabeth, *Sierra Leone*

I didn't think there were other alternatives at that time because there was no way to rescue myself at that moment. . . . there was no way to move out of that place because if you tried to force yourself to escape from Koidu you would be shot by ECOMOG [Economic Community of West African States Monitoring Group] troops. That was why we stayed on. They [the rebels] also warned us that if we tried to escape, we would be killed. ▪ Arthur, *Sierra Leone*

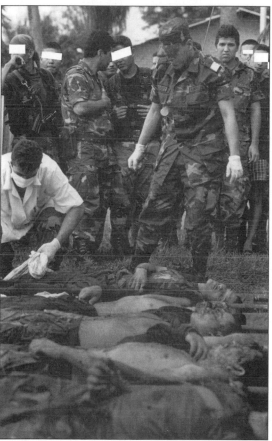

Young soldiers look upon the realities of war

Photo by T. Voeten

What this research shows is that frequently the distinction between voluntary and compulsory or forced recruitment is not clear-cut. Obviously there are degrees of "voluntariness." The young British 16- or 17-year-old volunteer soldier is not in the same situation as the young Afghan whose home area is invaded, or the young Sierra Leonean who is separated from home, family, and means of survival. Many young people are induced to join because they are told that they will be paid, or given other misleading information.

In addition, many who "volunteer" initially find that once in, there is little further opportunity to exercise choice about their continued participation. Some were misled by being told that they would be able to leave if they changed their mind. Others did not realize that this was not an activity that they could try out and then opt out of again if they changed their minds.

Whether they were forced or "volunteered," the effect of their experiences is profound and life-changing for these youngsters.[2] Those who identify themselves as having volunteered and end up committing repugnant acts may be burdened with the additional sense of guilt about the path they chose. Those who had no choice are also burdened by the horror of what they did and suffered: but know that they did not in any way choose this course. Some who made the choice, bitterly regret it. They may feel guilty for having run away from home and caused suffering to their families, as well as having the frustration of the wasted time in which they have lost educational opportunities. Where they feel they made a real choice and it was a huge mistake, they may find it difficult to trust their judgment in making further decisions.[3]

Legal Issues

Many of the experiences of these young soldiers raise points of law and legal issues. The ILO's Committee of Experts on the Application of Conventions and Recommendations[4] has considered a number of these in relation to forced labor, both generally and more specifically in relation to forced child labor, under the Forced Labour Convention, 1930 (No. 29).

The Committee of Experts has identified the following as factors indicative of forced labor in relation to adults,[5] which should therefore be considered as even more pertinent when applied to children:

• Misleading contracts, including "enticements"
• Ill-treatment inflicted on the worker, sometimes resulting in death

- Long working days of up to 18 hours without water or proper food
- No, or unreasonable restrictions on, freedom to terminate employment[6]

The Committee of Experts has dealt with the issue of child soldiers under Convention No. 29, but mostly in situations where the children were abducted or otherwise clearly physically forced.[7] However, when examining this Convention more generally in relation to children, the committee has identified the following amongst relevant factors:[8]

- Children being removed from their homes and families, and taken to a place unknown to them, where they find themselves isolated and forced to live and work in conditions that are much worse than those which they had been led to believe that they would experience
- Children being completely dependent upon their employers, no longer able to make any decisions regarding their own welfare, subject to the whims of the employer—in other words, their ability to make choices is removed from them
- Children becoming prisoners at the work sites, risking their lives if they try to flee

All of these factors should, therefore, be taken into account when considering the Worst Forms of Child Labour Convention, 1999 (No. 182), and the other international standards relating to military recruitment of children.

Legal issues surrounding voluntary recruitment only arise for those children over the age of 15, since no military recruitment or use of children under 15 years old in hostilities is permitted under any circumstances by anyone. This is not only a matter of international treaty law[9] but is also now recognized as international customary law. Therefore, as a matter of law, for children aged less than 15 years old at the time of recruitment, the question of whether or not they volunteered is irrelevant.

Equally, the question of distinguishing between voluntary recruitment and forced or compulsory recruitment does not arise for under-18s for those states that are parties to the African Charter on the Rights and Welfare of the Child (as of June 2003, there are 30 states parties to the Charter), since this requires these states to "take all necessary measures to ensure that no child [defined as less than 18 years old] shall take a direct part in hostilities and refrain, in particular, from recruiting any child."[10]

The Worst Forms of Child Labour Convention, 1999 (No. 182), prohibits "forced or compulsory labour, including forced or compulsory recruitment for use in armed conflict"[11] of children under 18 years. In addition, Convention No. 182 prohibits "work which, by its nature or the circumstances in which it is carried out, is likely to harm the health, safety or morals of children."[12] This is the only ILO standard specifically addressing the question of military recruitment of children. However, as this is identified as a form of forced labor it is necessary to consider what is meant by forced labor in the ILO's context, in particular as it relates to children. One effect of Convention No. 182 is to explicitly prohibit the conscription (legal compulsory recruitment) of under-18s, whereas Convention No. 29, Article 2, paragraph 2(a) excludes from the definition of forced labor (for the purposes of that Convention), "any work or service exacted in virtue of compulsory military service laws for work of a purely military character." Since the reporting process under Convention No. 182 has only begun recently, it will be important to take note of the Committee of Experts' comments relating to this issue.

The international community gave considerable attention to the question of distinguishing voluntary military recruitment from forced or compulsory recruitment during the drafting of the Optional Protocol to the Convention on the Rights of the Child on Involvement of Children in Armed Conflicts (2000).[13] However, the Protocol permits voluntary recruitment of under-18s only into government armed forces (not armed groups distinct from the armed forces of the state), and such voluntary recruitment may not in any case be below the age of 16.[14] It does not permit conscription of under-18s at all, or the direct use of under-18s in hostilities.

In order to ensure that volunteers below the age of 18 years are voluntary, the Protocol requires as a minimum that:

- Such recruitment is genuinely voluntary
- Such recruitment is carried out with the informed consent of the person's parents or legal guardians
- Such persons [potential recruits] are fully informed of the duties involved in such military service, and that
- Such persons provide reliable proof of age prior to acceptance into national military service

These conditions must *all* be met: they are cumulative, not alternatives. As a matter of international law, the Optional Protocol only applies where the state is a party to it. However, since these safeguards were considered to be essential for governments already committed not to send under-18s into combat, it is worth considering the Optional Protocol minimum safeguards as setting out baselines. If these criteria are not met the presumption should be that a recruit under the age of 18 must be considered not to have volunteered as a matter of law, even if they identify themselves as a volunteer.

The Optional Protocol safeguards fall into two groups: those that are clear and relatively precise, such as the requirements of proof of age and of parental or other legal consent; and those that are vaguer, or in the case of being "genuinely voluntary," self-evidently circular. ILO standards and their application over many years are especially relevant and helpful in relation to these two, less precise criteria in the Optional Protocol. The Committee on the Rights of the Child could usefully consider these standards and the ILO's jurisprudence when considering reports from states that are parties to the Optional Protocol.

Many of the young volunteers interviewed for this research project do not meet the criteria included in the Optional Protocol:

• Proof of age: only one of these self-defined volunteers indicated that their age had ever been a matter of concern to their recruiters (they tried to direct him into education instead).[15]

• Parental consent: many of these volunteers left without their parents' knowledge or contrary to their wishes (see box below).

• Potential recruits are fully informed of the duties involved in such military recruitment: it is evident that most of these young people had no real idea of what they were being asked to do. The fact that many would have left the armed forces or armed groups again but were unable to do so, strongly suggests that they were not "fully informed" of what the military recruitment entailed.

• The recruitment is genuinely voluntary. This criterion is not explained, but it would seem to indicate that there has to be some real objective measure of choice, physically and mentally. Each situation would, therefore, have to be judged on its facts. The example from Sierra Leone of those who did not join up being killed clearly indicates that any recruitment in these circumstances could not be considered "genuinely voluntary." Similarly, real questions arise where the under-18 wishes to leave the armed force or armed group but is unable to do so even if they apparently volunteered initially.

In this context, it is interesting to note that under the Protocol to Prevent, Suppress and Punish Trafficking in Persons, Especially Women

Parental Consent

Out of 53 interviewees, only 8 had the explicit prior consent of their parents to join up. Of the 29 young people that became involved without prior discussion with their parents, only 8 had their parents supporting them, and for 12 others the reaction was clearly negative:

My parents lived in the city, and I was in a boarding school. [. . .] My friends told my parents that I had joined. [. . .] After having heard this message, my dad had his first heart attack; he was transported to the hospital, and he died. He didn't agree.
■ Urbain, *DRC*

I went as a volunteer, without my father's authorization. He thought that my engagement was too serious. Considering that he knew how that happens in the army, he had to go through difficult times. He refused the idea that his children had a military career.
■ François, *Congo-Brazzaville*

The first time I went to the movement [. . .] I was brought back by my mother with a lot of difficulty. They initially protested because I had volunteered. She went there to protest and cried and cried and ultimately they gave me back. [. . .] Then again soon afterwards, I ran away again from home and joined the LTTE. [. . .] This time, I made sure that my mother could not trace me.
■ Gajathukan, *Sri Lanka*

My parents were totally against what I was doing.
■ Solomon, *South Africa*

My parents did not like us to speak about the politics, because they know this will end up, this will end up. . . with our deaths, with our killing. They were afraid of it. ■ Benny, *South Africa*

My parents wanted me to go to school. They were providing me with everything. [. . .] At first they disagreed with what I am doing. ■ Solomon, *South Africa*

I didn't discuss the matter with any family, but my mother did not like [me] to join the PAC. She was angry.
■ Ndeleni, *South Africa*

I left without saying a word to my family. ■ Vanessa, *DRC*

and Children, supplementing the UN Convention against Transnational Organized Crime, no one under the age of 18 years is considered to be capable of giving a valid consent to being trafficked.

Conclusion

As this research shows, many young people define themselves as volunteers although it is clear that objectively they had no real choice, and certainly that one or more of the Optional Protocol safeguards was not fulfilled. In many cases, the real circumstances clearly amount to forced labor.

Given the customary and treaty law prohibition on any recruitment or use in hostilities of under-15s, the question of voluntary recruitment of under-15s is irrelevant as a matter of law. All recruitment of any kind of under-18s and their use in hostilities by armed groups is unlawful. The same is true for state armies in the case of those states that are parties to the African Charter on the Rights and Welfare of the Child, or to the Optional Protocol if they have declared 18 or more as their minimum voluntary recruitment age.

For those young soldiers over 15 years old, in addition to considering each individual case on its merits, the presumption in any circumstances where the government is not clearly able and willing to comply with the Optional Protocol safeguards has to be that any under-18s were not recruited voluntarily, even if they define themselves as such. Moreover these safeguards should themselves be understood in the light of the accumulated experience in applying the concepts of forced labor and child labor.

However, the legality or otherwise of the recruitment has to be considered separately from the question of the approach to be taken in relation to designing and implementing practical programs to provide protection from and alternatives to such involvement, and in relation to demobilization, rehabilitation, and reintegration programs. Insofar as the young people themselves are concerned, if they consider that they volunteered, this has to be taken seriously in identifying the reasons why they joined and in planning how to address them whether as a preventative or a remedial measure.

Notes

1. Dumas and de Cock (2003) found significant differences in the numbers who said they volunteered between those who were still in armed forces or

armed groups and those who had left. Those still in tended to say they had volunteered. There are various possible reasons for this: they may have volunteered and that is why they are still in the armed forces or group; they may not want to reveal that they had been forcibly recruited; they may wish to be seen to be in control of their lives; or they may not have had time to reconsider the circumstances that led to their joining.

2. Commenting in the *British Medical Journal,* pediatricians D.G.H. de Silva and C. J. Hobbs suggest that "the involvement of dependent, developmentally immature children and adolescents in armed conflict they do not truly comprehend, to which they are unable to give informed consent, and which adversely affects the child's right to unhindered growth and identity" should be classified as child abuse (de Silva and Hobbs 2001, p. 1372).

3. Keairns 2002.

4. The Committee of Experts on the Application of Conventions and Recommendations (CEACR) is part of the regular machinery for supervision of ratified ILO Conventions. The Committee of Experts consists of 20 independent experts (mostly lawyers) and analyzes the law and practice in the light of the Convention's requirements. In the case of the Minimum Age Convention, 1973 (No. 138), and the Worst Forms of Child Labour Convention, 1999 (No. 182), governments must submit reports to the committee every two years regarding the application of the Conventions in their countries.

5. See *Report of the Committee of Experts on the Applications of Conventions and Recommendations,* Report III (Part 1A), International Labour Conference, Individual Observations concerning Convention No. 29, Forced Labour, 1930: Brazil (88th Session, 2000); Iraq (89th Session, 2001).

6. The CEACR has explicitly applied this "in time of peace, to career members of the armed forces, all of whom must remain free to terminate their employment by giving notice of reasonable length." (*Report of the Committee of Experts on the Applications of Conventions and Recommendations,* Report III [Part 1A], International Labour Conference, 89th Session, Individual Observations concerning Convention No. 29, Forced Labour, 1930: Iraq).

7. See CEACR comments: *Report of the Committee of Experts on the Applications of Conventions and Recommendations,* Report III (Part 1A), International Labour Conference, Individual Observations concerning Convention No. 29, Forced Labour, 1930: Sudan (85th Session, 1997); Burundi (90th Session, 2002); Democratic Republic of Congo (90th Session, 2002); Uganda (90th Session, 2002).

8. See CEARC comments presented in the *Report of the Committee of Experts on the Applications of Conventions and Recommendations,* Report III (Part 1A), for example, in 1998 in relation to teenage children working on fishing platforms in Indonesia; in 1995 (International Labour Conference, 82nd Session) in relation to forced child labor exploitation in Thailand; in 1993 (International Labour Conference, 80th Session) in relation to *restavek* children in domestic service in Haiti, and in 1992 (International Labour Conference, 79th Session) regarding labor practices in Brazil.

9. Convention on the Rights of the Child 1989; Additional Protocol I, 1977; Additional Protocol II, 1977; Rome Statute of the International Criminal Court, 1998.

10. African Charter on the Rights and Welfare of the Child, adopted by the Organization of African Unity in 1990, Article 22.

11. Ibid., Article 3(a).

12. Ibid., Article 3(d).

13. This Optional Protocol entered into force on 12 February 2002 and 54 states are already parties to it (as of 30 July 2003).

14. Because of the dispute between those states that wished to prohibit *all* recruitment and use of under-18s, and those states that wished to continue recruiting under-18s as volunteers into their armed forces, the provision is more complex, since states have to make a legally binding declaration on ratification or accession specifying their minimum voluntary recruitment age, which may not be less than 16 years. Thus many of the states parties have specified a minimum age of 18 years, or higher, while others have declared it as 17 or 16 years.

15. It can be assumed that this is not an issue in relation to the armed forces of the United Kingdom where age is checked routinely as part of the process, but the question did not come up in the interviews.

7

Conclusion

I personally believe that when people are young, others can abuse them. It is my very unfortunate fate that I was drawn into wars. If instead of war skills, I knew other skills and knowledge, now I could use my knowledge and expertise. Then today I would be an engineer or doctor or something else useful for my society and myself. If I knew some skills I could contribute to solve our problems and I could help others. For instance, now many Afghan children are illiterate and if I was able to teach I could teach some of them. It is my wish to teach at least alphabets to our children, to teach literacy to some 40 or 50 children. This was rather better for us than getting involved in war. ▪ Javad, *Afghanistan*

The dilemma of child combatants must rise where on one hand the situation is so bleak that one has no economic or political opportunities and on the other hand they lack access to education.
▪ (Reflection of a *Pakistan* interviewer)

I have lost my chance to get education; the time has passed now. It was my dream to get education and lead a successful life but my dream of becoming a teacher remained unfulfilled.
▪ Aziz, *Pakistan*

I want to advise people who want to be rebel fighters, young soldiers, that they should learn from that we have gone through which is too sad an experience. Those children younger than we are should never again be involved in such a life anymore. [. . .] What I have seen and undergone is not for a child to experience.
▪ Arthur, *Sierra Leone*

The purpose of this study was to identify the risk factors leading to adolescent "voluntary" recruitment from the standpoint of the young people who volunteer themselves, and thus to help in the planning of sustainable demobilization and reintegration for such young soldiers, with a view to preventing re-recruitment. Given the nature of the study and its findings, it is not proposed to provide an extensive list of detailed recommendations for prevention, disarmament, demobilization, rehabilitation, reintegration, and prevention of re-recruitment. Instead the recommendations focus on the key points that need to be considered, taking account of the factors that render young people vulnerable to involvement.

What this research shows is that although there will always be individual exceptions, there are certain underlying factors without which young people are unlikely to become involved in armed forces or armed groups. The same factors, but in more specific form and in combination, make some young people more likely to join than their peers. Then there are certain trigger events that lead to the actual decision to join. Many young people think about joining for years before actually doing so. Many others think about it, but never join.

These factors are both cumulative and related in complex direct and indirect ways. A surprising number are common to all the situations featured in this research, despite the wide differences in geography, socio-economic development, culture, and religion. They provide a framework of issues that should always be considered in planning for both prevention of recruitment and for demobilization and reintegration. At the same time, it is essential to analyze each of these factors in the particular situation under consideration in order to take account of the degree, weight, nature, and particularities of the impact these risk factors have in that situation. More importantly, the same "solutions" cannot be applied generically even within one situation, because of the differences within a country, and because of the different individuals and groups involved—boys and girls, rural and urban, those with and those without families to return to, or to support, and so on. Thus the framework of risk factors identified in this study applies at each level of analysis and planning of the policy and programs themselves.

Although this study focuses on one aspect of "child soldiering," the issue needs to be considered in the broader context of child labor, of which it is in effect a specialized branch. Thus actions that minimize the likelihood of child labor will also reduce child soldiering, and addressing only the specifics of child soldiering will tend to increase other forms of child labor. A classic illustration of this is the situation of girl soldiers whose limited alternatives to soldiering, both initially and after demobilization, could push them toward prostitution.

The key factors making these young people vulnerable to military participation reflect the particular situation of adolescents. As an age group they attend school in fewer numbers than younger children; this is true even more so in the case of adolescent girls. They find themselves heading households and taking on adult responsibilities while having lower earning power and missing out on traditional opportunities to learn a trade, and adolescent girls are more likely to be sexually abused.[1] At the same time, they have capabilities: they are physically stronger than younger children and are, therefore, more prone to be targets for all forms of work, including military recruitment; they have ideas, imagination, commitment, and the capacity to take independent action.

Key Factors

The key factors identified in this research are war, family, education and employment, poverty, and the peer group.

War

One of the most significant and yet least-considered aspects of this issue in all respects is war itself. Few young people go looking for a war to join; for many, war comes to them and becomes part of their normal environment. With it, war brings insecurity. It causes schools to close; impoverishes and disrupts families through death, injury, and displacement; and leaves few avenues of employment other than military ones. The presence of war creates military role models and status symbols far beyond the conflict area itself, and validates violence as a means of protection. These are all background factors that can encourage participation, but they impact particularly on adolescents, for whom family, school, and role models are especially strong influences. For them, war, whether at home or abroad, may provide an opportunity: many adolescents are running away from domestic exploitation or abuse.

It is therefore self-evident that eliminating armed conflicts would be the single most effective means of preventing youth participation. Thus all measures aimed at addressing the causes of conflicts, of peace building, nonviolent conflict resolution, and peaceful settlement of disputes, as well as bringing existing conflicts to an end, should be strenuously sought. Young people should be specifically included in these processes. At the same time, there are many steps that can be taken before, during, and after armed conflicts to reduce the likelihood of young people being involved. Many of these are addressed under separate headings, although caused or exacerbated by war, or otherwise interrelated. At the same time, any means of discouraging military and political leaders from deliberately seeking to recruit young people would also be helpful. This is where a strong legal framework is important, including criminal penalties for recruiters.

Family

Next to war, the family is the major factor influencing whether young people do or do not become involved in the armed forces or armed groups. The absence of family is a crucial predictor of recruitment or embroilment in armed conflict. It has already been documented[2] that children separated from their family, for whatever reasons and whether permanently or temporarily, are the most vulnerable to both forced and voluntary recruitment by all parties to armed conflicts. It emerges from this study that this is indeed a crucial factor, specifically in relation to the voluntary recruitment of adolescents. Therefore, whatever stops the separation of the young person from the actual family environment is likely to reduce child recruitment. Such obvious basic facts present significant challenges in developing appropriate strategies. This conclusion does, however, underline the importance of programs, long-term or emergency, that stress the importance of keeping families together and prioritize family reunification.

Where the family is involved in the conflict or has a military tradition, the involvement of the children is more likely because it is expected (at least of boys), is more likely to be seen as an option by the young people, and is more likely to meet with parental approval.

By contrast, an abusive or exploitative family situation emerges as the significant factor in the individual decision to leave home and join up. This is the single greatest cause for girls who face sexual as well as physical abuse and domestic exploitation of their labor, although many boys are also running away from physical abuse by a parent. Adolescence is a time when there is likely to be greater vulnerability to such exploitation or abuse because of the intergenerational power struggle, the difficulties of puberty for both the child and the parent, with its physical and emotional challenges, and the young person's wish for greater autonomy and independence. These are exacerbated by the breakup and/or reconstitution of families, and the additional social and economic tensions and problems brought about by war.

Parents should be responsible for their children—they should love them and send them to school. I left and joined the NPA [New People's Army] because I wanted to run away from my family's noise and I hated getting hurt. ▪ Sonia, *Philippines*[3]

This diagnosis, and the plea from the young people themselves, present severe challenges, but not ones that can be avoided if the voluntary participation of adolescents is actually to be addressed. There are at least three separate aspects. The first of these is the need to improve parenting skills and reduce domestic violence in general. The devastating impact of interpersonal violence and the need to respond to it is only just being recognized.[4] Second, there is the specific need to address the situation and treatment of girls within the family. Although children of both sexes are liable to physical abuse, girls are more likely to be sexually abused than boys, and are also more likely to be expected to stay at home to undertake domestic chores, or to be sent to their extended family for this purpose. This links with the third aspect: the need to address more generally the status and treatment of girls (and women) in society. Perversely, the broader challenge may be easier in one sense because it falls within the public rather than the private domain and so is more accessible to public policy responses such as linking it to girls' access to education, employment, skills, and leadership positions. An even greater effect in reducing adolescent volunteering would result from addressing the gender stereotyping of boys that encourages or pressures them into going into armed forces or armed groups.

Because this study focuses on adolescents who joined armed forces or armed groups, the positive role of the family in *preventing* recruitment has been understated. It is clear that a positive family ambience that opposes the children becoming involved in the conflict or in the military is the single strongest preventive factor. A high priority should therefore be to reinforce the general capacity of families to survive—economically, physically, and emotionally—and for parents to understand the impact of involvement in conflict on children, and thus themselves to act as deterrents to volunteering.

Education and Employment

Both the access to and the content of education are significant factors in the lives and decisions of adolescents.

As I know, education is the key. It is better than silver and gold.
▪ Augustine, *Sierra Leone*

Young people who are excluded from education—whether because of poverty, closure of schools, or bad behavior—have to find something else to do. Those without adequate and appropriate schooling are limited in their employment choices. When the army is a major employer and requires no educational attainments, its availability is a major factor. This is true in peacetime but tends to be magnified during armed conflicts as alternative forms of economic activity for young people—even those with education—become increasingly limited and the army or armed groups become larger in themselves and more significant as the source of economic opportunity or advancement.

> *So, in an area where economic opportunities are scarce, education is not free, where no law can be extended, [and] the border area has been at war for the last 24 years: could one expect some positive changes other than fighting Jihad?* ▪ (Reflection of a *Pakistan* interviewer.)

For those excluded from school on behavioral grounds, belonging to an armed group may not only be attractive in itself, but may also be a form of self-protection, particularly where the exclusion was linked to violent behavior and/or involvement with weapons. The army or armed group may also provide status, a sense of belonging, and economic survival or advancement, as well as simply something to do.

Schools provide many opportunities to influence young people. This may be through a deliberate recruitment strategy by the regular armed forces—through gaining access to schools by offering classes, using the schools for advertising, cadet or other military training programs, or through offering to pay for further education or training. Schools may also be used to encourage students to join the "armed struggle" in the name of liberation, religion, ethnicity, or some other cause. The school environment provides a fertile ground because it links the teacher-pupil relationship with peer-group pressure, and may also minimize (or reinforce) family influence. Schooling that is segregated on racial, religious, linguistic or other grounds can be a factor in exacerbating tensions in society because it fosters the isolation of these groups, even apart from any particular content in the education itself. However, for young people the schooling system may also be a major point of impact of what they see as an oppressive regime, and may thus in itself become a major cause and fertile breeding ground of resistance. In addition to these general issues, specific personal humiliations, denigration, bullying, and corporal punishment all impact on young people who are going through the adolescent stage of insecurity linked to rebellion, and make them more vulnerable to seeking alternative support structures.

It is therefore essential to provide education for children and young people that is accessible and affordable, in a setting where they are not beaten, humiliated, or bullied, and that encourages and promotes nonviolent and nonmilitaristic approaches, attitudes, and role models. The school's curriculum and the attitudes fostered there should be designed to counter the popular mythology of the heroism and glamour of war, and help pupils to understand the realities behind the images. At the same time, teaching young people to resolve interpersonal conflicts nonviolently not only reinforces these values but also aids them in staying out of trouble at home and outside, and starts building the parenting skills for the next generation.

At the same time, the educational system needs to be adapted to the employment situation. The disenchantment of educated youth without employment, or the prospect of it, is a factor distinct from the frustrations of those without education.

Poverty

The single most commonly identifiable characteristic of child soldiers (of all ages) is poverty. Poverty—and the need for personal or family survival—is a risk factor that can drive young people into armed forces and armed groups to provide food and financial support, either formally or informally. At the same time, poverty can be an indirect cause of recruitment, such as preventing access to education. Even where schooling is free, the young person may be deterred from attending because of the inability to purchase school materials (pens, books, and so forth) or adequate clothing or shoes. At the same time, the family may need the additional earning power of the young person, or may need an older child to stay at home to look after younger siblings.

Any effective poverty reduction measures are, therefore, helpful. More specifically, identifying poverty in relation to the other risk factors or categories would enable the development of more specific and targeted responses. Examples might be encouraging school attendance through practical measures such as providing free school meals, providing child-care facilities, identifying and following up on children who drop out of school, whether temporarily or permanently, and looking for alternatives that enable the children to enter or continue in education. At the same time, it is important to recognize and address the way in which war tends to increase both poverty and vulnerability in other respects, by making efforts to keep education going and accessible—including to displaced and refugee children—and by identifying and addressing economic, social, and other barriers. The particular focus on adolescent vulnerability makes it imperative that "education" is not interpreted as referring only to primary education.

Poverty is also relative. While income levels in the industrialized nations are far above those of developing countries, young people from low-income households or who are otherwise socially marginalized have severely reduced options in terms of both education and employment, and these same issues need to be addressed.

The linkages between poverty, education, and employment or other viable economic activities are complex and need to be factored into policy planning in realistic and practical ways. The experience of addressing other forms of child labor could provide useful models or parallels.

Peer Groups and Other Social Influences

The influence of the peer group—friends, school companions—and the search for status and "acceptable" role models is the other group of key factors in influencing young people to join armed forces or armed groups. In many situations, adolescents encourage each other to do things, including seeking adventure or defining their own role models. Sometimes a group of friends or a whole class joins up together. Where having a gun or being in uniform are perceived as desirable, these will be significant factors, in particular where the opportunity to do so is readily available. Culture and tradition, and the media, may also portray these elements as positive or something to aspire to, giving them greater importance than such basic goals as having sufficient food, money, a family, or self-protection. Where these images and role models are filtered and reinforced by school and family their influence is magnified.

The Right to Leave

This study focuses on adolescents who defined themselves as having volunteered to join armed forces or armed groups. The concept of voluntary recruitment is normally considered in the light of the initial method of joining. Many of the young people interviewed for this research did not join as the result of a considered exercise of decision-making taken in the light of viable alternatives. Although they defined themselves as "volunteers," the actual degree of choice varies from those situations where the "choice" was (directly or indirectly) between joining and likely death or physical or sexual violence, through those where joining was seen as a ticket to food or economic survival of self or family, to situations where a significant measure of choice was indeed exercised. However, even in the latter cases, many young people joined believing that they could "try out" this option, with little appreciation of the likely effects of the experience. Moreover, few of them realized that, in most instances, if they joined there would be no possibility of leaving again unless they escaped in peril of their lives. The impulsive nature of adolescence, and the lack of understanding of the reality and serious consequences of their involvement in armed forces or armed groups, call into question the idea of a clear, hard-and-fast distinction between voluntary and compulsory or forced recruitment of young people in this age group. Claims of voluntary recruitment should be treated with critical scepticism.

Improving Socioeconomic Reintegration

There are many challenges for successful long-term socioeconomic reintegration of adolescent volunteer soldiers that emerge from this study. Three of the most significant are education, employment or other viable economic activity, and the reestablishment of relations with their families. Each of these will be considered below, but it is important to stress that in planning all reintegration programs, the young soldiers themselves should be consulted. Furthermore, it is essential that the gender dimensions of socioeconomic reintegration are taken into account. If reintegration is linked to demobilization, the first step is to ensure that girls as well as boys are able, both in theory and in practice, to access the demobilization process. At the same time, in situations where girls themselves may not wish to be identified as having been associated with armed forces or armed groups because of societal attitudes and the likely implications for their future, socioeconomic programs need to be more broadly available. In this way, the needs of those girls who want recognition of their role and of those who do not can both be accommodated. In all aspects of socioeconomic reintegration, the different needs of boys and girls should be taken into account, since their actual situations, prospects, and societal roles may be significantly different.

Education

Education is clearly a priority for many of these young soldiers. Not only can it play a role in preventing initial recruitment, but it can also help to avoid re-recruitment and presents these young people with alternatives for their futures, thus aiding reintegration.

> *Well, I need a scholarship towards my education [he was a signaler for the RUF during the war and now wants to be a journalist]. We need our school to be rebuilt and to increase the furniture that was there during the normal days before the war so that our school activities can go on normally again.* ▪ Augustine, *Sierra Leone*

> *The main thing for our reintegration to be better is for school materials to be issued to us to further our education and if there will be any support like microcredit to our parents and for scholarships to those that . . . That is the main thing that can help the reintegration to succeed.* ▪ Arthur, *Sierra Leone*

As these young people indicate, educational opportunities do not just require the existence of schools, but also the ability of pupils to support themselves, or the capacity of their families to support them, while they receive education. The particular problems and questions relating to formal education, vocational training, and apprenticeships

Photo by G. Cabrera

Education and employment opportunities mitigate adolescents' need to "volunteer"

and similar schemes all need to be taken into account. In each situation, the priorities of girls and boys in relation to formal education, vocational training, or direct access to apprenticeships or employment may differ.

Again, it is no good if education is available in theory if former child soldiers encounter disincentives to enrolling. Where girls have babies, they may encounter obstacles not only because of the need for child care and financial support for themselves and the baby, but also because in normal circumstances pregnant girls or those with babies may be routinely excluded from school.

Solomon (South Africa) found himself excluded from the free education program because when living with his grandmother he was unwilling to reveal that he had been in exile:

> *People, they don't know me, [and] I don't want people to have those fears: "Hey, did you kill people? Hey, you are one of those guerrillas!"*

It is, however, not only the real, effective access to school that is important, but also the quality of the educational experience, and its relevance to perceived future or even present economic prospects:

> *In 1997, there was an order of release, in order to return to school [. . .] but I wanted to do something else in order to secure my future; there are two younger ones after me, so I have to do something.*
> ■ Germain, DRC

This is a salutary reminder that these young people often were ones who in any case had sought to take control of their lives, and even to take responsibility for other members of the family. Thus for many of them, to go back to school "like children" is neither economically nor emotionally a real option without strong economic and societal support. Furthermore, although all these young people joined as adolescents, by the time of demobilization and reintegration many "child soldiers" will in fact be adults.

This does not alter the basis and nature of their adolescent armed experience, but may disguise it. They may look like adults and even behave like adults, at least superficially. However, their needs, may be more akin to those of children since they too missed out on education, were separated from families, and so on.[5] Programs addressed solely to those still under 18 at the time of demobilization will, therefore, overlook many young people who were recruited and fought as child soldiers. This is one of the places at which the broader definition of "youth" as up to the age of 25 may well be a more appropriate category.

More specifically, the young people may feel unable to go back home empty-handed. The DRC interviewer comments that many think of joining another armed group in order to earn money, and adds that "many Kadogos are bitter concerning their current situation. It is this bitterness, this feeling of being misled, which brought a Kadogo belonging to the presidential guard to assassinate President Kabila in January 2001."

> *They promised to send us to school to study, [and now] they owe us money, somewhere between $3,000 and $5,000 each . . . when we enrolled, they made a promise to us.* ▪ Germain, *DRC*

Employment

Education is expected to lead to employment. To provide employment or other economically productive activity for young people not only fulfills the essential requirement of giving them things to do, social status, and a social network, it also helps to ensure that they and their families have at the least a means of survival and preferably a reasonable standard of living. Without them, what is the prospect facing a former child soldier?

> *There is that little bit of regret because I can see today I am doing nothing. I am not working and also I am suffering more than before.*
> ▪ Benny, *South Africa*

> *I had a child because I could not protect myself from a boy. . . . I have to learn a job, so that I can work and earn money for my son. I want to do things; I don't want to go and live in the street.*
> ▪ Christine, *DRC*

At the same time, employment-related interventions need to be backed up by special activities encouraging trust and the development of healthy social values. The mental scars from conflict experiences mark the character and personality of these young people, making their reintegration more complicated than that of adult ex-combatants.[6]

It is perhaps hardest for those who fought for a cause—for liberation—and then find themselves in no better situation afterwards. For those who joined because there were no other choices at that time, it is also difficult but there is less of a sense of having been "let down" by the new authorities. Some feel that they were better off in the army, while recognizing that there are also benefits of being out, such as better protection. This comes through strongly from both East Timor and South Africa. This is not a criticism of the governments concerned, who face enormous difficulties in establishing education, employment, and other economic activities for all, not just for those who missed out on education because of their involvement in the liberation struggle. Nevertheless, it reflects the reality as the young people themselves see it. In East Timor, many of the youth who were involved in the clandestine movement are turning to alcohol and aggression because they no longer have a direction:

The situation has made them like that because they don't have any money or employment. [. . .] People have no chance to get an education because schooling is very expensive and their parents have to find money. ▪ Helena, *East Timor*

But the best I need [. . .] is the skill, because military skills are no longer valuable in peacetime. [. . .] I feel myself like—what is it?— something you can take and then throw it away.
▪ Benny, *South Africa*

My parents, what are they saying? "You have been there and what have you gained from it? [. . .] You are still here, living at the back of our home." [. . .] My parents make me feel as if my efforts were useless. [Serious] But I know it from inside that they are still going to see it, even if it is the generations to come. ▪ Solomon, *South Africa*

I have no money, no job, no nothing. [. . .] I wanted to be a mechanic. I wanted to fix cars, buses—but now it's almost impossible because if I want to have training to be a mechanic, I need money, and I don't have money. ▪ Pierre, *Congo-Brazzaville*

For those like Ali (Afghanistan), who contributed so much and seemed to have a bright future, but have been disabled as a result of their war experience, both education and job prospects are even more restricted. The feeling of not contributing to family and society may be enhanced by the sense of being a burden on them.

In particular, the "suspended animation" of prolonged demobilization without an income or future can leave these young combatants angry, disillusioned, and frustrated, and pulls some of them back into the army or into armed groups. Although they now know what they are getting into, some at least feel that this enables them to earn an income and take charge of their lives, rather than sitting around:

> *Currently, it's destabilization; what I want to say, it's that in the army, I suffered, but I had a home, a place to stay; I could organize myself, I ate. It's not like where we are now . . . I would like to flee, you know, some children fled so as not to be demobilized . . . some stay a month here, and then they run away.* ▪ Michel, DRC

> *At least in the army, we had money, we received wages. But since we're here, nothing.* ▪ Christine, DRC

This is a sharp reminder of the need to keep in mind the cyclical nature of the vulnerability factors and the importance of effective sustainable reintegration in order to prevent re-recruitment. For girls who were seeking equality or a nontraditional role through participation in the armed forces or armed groups, "reintegration" into a society that has not changed may feel like a step backward rather than a step forward. There is also a second-generation aspect. Although not all former girl soldiers have babies, many do.

Up to now, too little attention has been given to issues about marriage—validation or not of "war-time" marriages; supportive demobilization processes for those girls with babies who are still in a relationship with the boy-soldier father; as well as access for girls to education, vocational training, and employment. For girls, these difficulties will be compounded by the likelihood of them having babies to cope with as well, the societal attitudes toward girl soldiers, and their own possible desire for nontraditional employment—such as metalworking or even joining/continuing in the armed forces. However, consideration also needs to be given to the impact on the baby: if the demobilized girl soldier is not able to continue her education, to survive economically, and to establish a good family environment for the growing child, the vulnerability factors are being created for the next generation of young soldiers.

Family Reunification

Although it is well understood that family reunification is a crucial element in the rehabilitation and reintegration of child soldiers, even in situations where it was not anticipated it has been found to be the most important factor for demobilized young soldiers.[7] At the same time, for many of these young people it is a problematic issue. After all, as demonstrated earlier, many of them ran away from home in the first place because they were physically or sexually abused. Others had no family left. Even if the family still exists and can be traced, and even if they would like to return home, what prospects does it offer them now?

> *If our parents are dead what will we do, and then what will we do when we'll be back home? They are going to leave us over there without anything, without work.* ▪ Vanessa, DRC

For these older "young soldiers," therefore, the possibility of re-establishing links with their families may be important, but it cannot on its own be the answer. At the same time, some of them are desperate to go home, to make amends to their families, to reestablish contact. This still does not alter the reality that they cannot simply live at home. Even if the family relationships are improved, whether because of the absence or the change in age, maturity, and circumstances of the young person, what are they going to do? An analysis of a sample of fathers and sons before, during, and after recruitment/nonrecruitment into armed conflict suggests that the relationship in fact changes little in the different phases: thus the poor or nonexistent relationship continues, and on demobilization the same problems are likely to arise without external intervention, such as counseling.[8] At best, for these young people family reunification may be an important step, but it is only one step.

What Prospects?

Perhaps because these young people were indeed those who made choices, the strength of character and survival skills that they demonstrate is both a cause for celebration and a cause for concern about the societies that gave them this option. In the most difficult situations, many of these young people have demonstrated a commitment to "humanitarian values" and a lack of vindictiveness that shame adults. Their determination to better themselves and others deserves to be supported: these young people have and can continue to provide leadership, inspiration, and skills for their societies in the future if they are given the opportunity. In so doing, it is of course equally important to give these chances to those who in similar circumstances chose not to join. However, as this research has clearly demonstrated, if the critical issues that lead young people to join armed forces or armed groups were to be addressed, this would equally benefit other children and young people as well.

Unfortunately, in the end, it is equally clear that as long as wars continue, and in particular civil wars, children and young people will become soldiers.

> *As long as there is war here in the Congo, I don't think that children will stop joining up.* ▪ Germain, *DRC*

This is not an excuse for doing nothing. Rather it highlights the importance of addressing the factors that lead to child participation in a consistent, integrated, and coherent fashion and at both macro and micro levels, while also working to relieve the reasons that cause armed conflicts to occur and to persuade the parties to resolve their disputes through social dialogue and other nonviolent means.

> *The leaders of the country don't help us, because they always want to give out weapons; we, we want peace now. We, the young people of today, we want peace. We want to inform ourselves, we don't want the war. . . . We are all the children of the same country. The war isn't good. We want peace in Congo. The leaders should put their children on the front line, so that they will be destroyed. The weapons should be used to protect the nation, not to kill our brothers.*
> ▪ Pascal, *Congo-Brazzaville*

Notes

1. Women's Commission for Refugee Women and Children 2000, pp. 4–5.
2. Brett and McCallin 1998.
3. Camacho, Balanon, and Verba 2001, p. 22.
4. The World Health Organization recently issued the first ever *World Report on Violence and Health,* and in May 2003 the World Health Assembly unanimously adopted a resolution calling for urgent action to stem the global public-health impact of violence. The United Nations is currently undertaking a high-level expert study on violence against children.
5. Richards 2002, p. 274.
6. Achio and Specht 2003, p. 158.
7. UNICEF 2000.
8. Dumas and de Cock 2003, pp. 58–59.

APPENDIX I

Research and Methodological Issues

This appendix will provide the reader with the essential background information on the original project proposal and its objectives, the methodology used for the selection of case studies and informants, the methodology of data collection for this book—including the topic list for open interviewing and some statistics on the primary data—and finally on the way the materials have been analyzed, interpreted, and presented.

The Project Proposal

The research reported in this book was conducted as a joint project of the Quaker United Nations Office, Geneva, and the ILO Infocus Programme on Crisis Response and Reconstruction (IFP/CRISIS), with funding from the Ministry of Foreign Affairs of the Kingdom of the Netherlands. The following text provides the summary of the research project as it was originally designed.

Goal

To deepen the understanding of the root causes of children joining armed forces or armed groups in order to improve the knowledge base needed for the development of effective socioeconomic reintegration programs.

Objectives

1. To contribute to the understanding of the root causes of the phenomenon of children participating in armed conflict

137

2. To develop the knowledge of and discussion about voluntary recruitment of youth into armed forces or armed groups
3. To identify the issues for sustainable reintegration
4. To disseminate the information to those who need it
5. To improve public awareness about the reasons why youth join armed forces and armed groups

Rationale

In most of today's conflicts children become fighters. Some are abducted or otherwise physically forced to join armed forces or armed groups. Many others join without physical coercion. Although some demobilization and reintegration of these children takes place following a peace agreement and actual settlement of the conflict, in many situations it is taking place in unstable circumstances or while the conflict is continuing. In particular in the latter situations, unless the reasons why children become involved are addressed, the demobilization and reintegration programs are unlikely to be successful or sustained: even if they temporarily return to civilian life, the children are likely to be drawn back into the conflict. It is therefore essential to understand the reasons that the children themselves identify for joining armed forces or armed groups, whether by individual choice or as a result of other factors.

Methodology

In order to understand the reasons that the young soldiers themselves identify as the factors for their joining the armed forces or armed groups, the research will be undertaken in the form of in-depth individual interviews of the young people. Although ILO Convention No. 182 and the Convention on the Rights of the Child define all those up to 18 years as "children," since this study is focused on adolescent soldiers specifically, the terms "youth" and "young soldiers" are used as being more appropriate. In order to ensure that different countries and cultures are taken into account, the objective is to conduct case studies in at least five countries with a minimum of five respondents in each. Three taped interviews should be conducted with each respondent. The results of these interviews will be analyzed by the project supervisors, and supplemented by material from existing literature and other sources.

Outcome

1. An attractive and easy-to-read book presenting the results of the research drawing extensively on the responses of the interviewees themselves
2. A report and other publications with a broader analysis of the themes identified and the socioeconomic reintegration policy and programmatic responses needed as a result for policymakers in governmental, intergovernmental, and nongovernmental forums
3. Presentations of these materials and results in workshops, meetings, and publications

The Case Studies

It cannot be claimed that the young people interviewed in this research are a representative sample of the child soldiers of the world, although deliberate efforts were made to go outside the usually reported situations (hence, in particular, the inclusion of case studies of Congo-Brazzaville, the United Kingdom, and Afghans in Iran), and some regional balance has been ensured.

While seeking to obtain maximum diversity, the definition of the case studies was partly driven by the practical considerations of identifying and enrolling appropriately qualified researchers and obtaining appropriate contacts with potential interviewees. This is an important fact because the anthropological, qualitative nature of this study makes it essential to do this kind of research only with researchers that already have an established network on the ground or are in a position to develop one and can build up relationships of trust in these politically highly sensitive contexts.

Members or recent members of armed forces and armed groups are not easy subjects for study. They tend to be found in places that are hazardous to visit. They themselves may be dangerous for a researcher who is, for whatever reason, unable to establish the necessary rapport. There may be resistance from the organization to which they belong, or belonged, because of the danger of their revealing sensitive information or because by speaking as individuals they breach the culture of facelessness that, whether in long military traditions or in revolutionary cells, can be seen as an important element of solidarity and discipline. If recruitment has in practice taken place below the legal permissible age, or there is any feeling of political sensitivity about recruitment ages, this hesitancy is obviously compounded. Such reactions can prevent in-depth interviews from taking place, can in one way or another constrain the ability of the interviewee to speak freely, or can put interviewers, interviewees, and sometimes others at physical risk. All of these considerations were addressed in the detailed research methodology. It should not be imagined that the various dangers referred to are trivial; any of them could, at worst, be fatal.

In terms of setting up the project, all of this meant that it was not possible to make a purely scientific decision as to which countries or groups were most deserving of study, and proceed from there. Practical considerations had to intervene. In the event, the planned interviews in the Goma region of the DRC had to be aborted because of the security situation. Nor did it prove possible to obtain the desired interviews from young people associated with Republican (i.e., Catholic) groups in Northern Ireland. Other constraints meant that only two interviews were obtained for the United Kingdom government armed forces.

Although there are two instances where the situations overlap,[1] each of the nine case studies was discrete. The case studies in the Republic of Congo (Congo-Brazzaville) and the Democratic Republic of Congo (where there is no overlap), have been carried out by the same researcher; otherwise, each case study was the work of a different researcher, working independently within the general project guidelines.

Since the purpose of this research was to understand why adolescents volunteer for armed forces and armed groups, it was important to consider different kinds of situations. The United Kingdom recruits thousands of 16- and 17-year-old volunteers each year and, until 1 September 2002, routinely sent under-18s into combat. These young soldiers therefore fell squarely within the framework of this research, which was concerned with the reasons for joining rather than questions of legality and otherwise. Were this research focused on comparing the different case studies, the two interviews with young British soldiers obviously could not stand alone. Similarly, were the interviews being treated as throwing up data for quantitative analysis, the disproportionate representation of Europe among members of regular armed forces interviewed would have to be considered an unacceptable skewing of the sample.

In qualitative research, by contrast, informants are generally chosen. Choosing the informants on the basis of a number of different criteria (as explained above) has the advantage of selecting those people that are most knowledgeable, or that might be to a certain extent "typical" of a specific subcategory of subjects (such as girl soldiers, or soldiers from government or paramilitary groups). Within the qualitative framework of this research project, the two sets of interviews from soldiers in the British army represent, therefore, extra information from different valuable perspectives. It is essential to the accurate reporting of the project that they are included in order not to retrospectively misrepresent the approach and assumptions underlying the research, and also not to arbitrarily discard *any* material that was produced. Accordingly, material from the interview with these two young men is scattered through the report along with that from the other interviews and it is for the reader to judge the extent to which these vindicate the search for common features independent of cultural context.

A pilot study was conducted in South Africa in October and November 2001, involving interviews with six veterans of Umkhonto wa Sizwe and the Azanian People's Liberation Army, the principal armed groups that had been involved in the liberation struggle. The methodology was slightly changed after this pilot study, and nine further case studies were undertaken between May 2002 and February 2003, as follows:

Afghanistan: five interviewees, from various factions, interviewed as refugees in Iran

Colombia: seven interviewees, principally from the FARC and the AUC "paramilitaries"

Congo-Brazzaville: five interviewees, principally from the "Cobra" and "Ninja" factions, including one now in the government armed forces

Democratic Republic of Congo: seven interviewees, from various factions of the Alliance of Democratic Forces for the Liberation of Congo-Zaire (AFDL) which became the government under Laurent Kabila

Pakistan: five interviewees who had fought for the Taliban in Afghanistan

Sierra Leone: five interviewees, from government, opposition, and civil defense forces

Sri Lanka: seven interviewees from the LTTE

United Kingdom (Northern Ireland): four interviewees associated with "Protestant/Loyalist" factions

United Kingdom (British Army): two interviewees, serving soldiers, contacted through the army itself

Including the pilot study, this book thus presents selections of 53 interviews, in four continents (and seven distinct regions).

Selection of Informants

This book has managed to feature at least some respondents from each of the principal situations in which "child soldiers" can be found: government armed forces; opposition armed groups (including some that have been successful and assumed the mantle of government); a variety of local defense groups ranging from the overtly state-sponsored to the completely informal, through those whose status and allegiance remains unclear; ideological movements calling on volunteers from countries outside the immediate conflict zone; and, finally, some armed gangs that qualify as players on the political scene, rather than a purely criminal phenomenon, by virtue of their claimed agenda or their effective control of territory. Furthermore, some interviewees served in more than one group.

The "informants" approach is a widely used survey methodology in socioeconomic disciplines. The selection process of the informants in this study has followed this methodology. In fact, as all people interviewed were (ex) child soldiers themselves, rather than people who knew a lot about them, the approach taken in this study is a variant of the well-known "key informants approach." Key informants were used to identify the children and to establish and verify the background of the children and the interview situation. The selection of informants has also been subject to a number of practical issues, namely the established network of the researchers and the accessibility of the children in terms of security. However, the research guide specially developed for this project clearly encouraged the researchers to find a varied sample of interviewees: male and female; those still serving; those who were officially demobilized and those who "auto-demobilized"; those who fight/fought with government forces, with armed opposition groups, and armed groups not opposing the government; those with frontline experience and those who have performed exclusively support roles; those from urban and rural backgrounds; and members of as many different ethnic and religious communities as possible. Some fuller details of the variables of the respondents are given below under the heading of "Primary Data."

In fact, the greatest bias in the sample is the underrepresentation of young people who served in *regular* governmental armed forces. Contrary to popular perceptions, this category represents the majority of "child soldiers" as defined using the threshold age of 18 generally recognized as the age of majority.[2] However, access to serving and former soldiers in "regular" armed forces is particularly problematic. From this point of view, the authors are especially grateful to the British Army Training and Recruiting Agency for arranging interviews with serving soldiers who had been recruited below the age of 18. It is understandable that while granting permission the army would wish to exercise some control over which "voices" were heard; thus the interviewees were "satisfied soldiers" who had volunteered to work in army recruitment offices.

Within each case study the interviewees are in practice those who were accessible and willing to talk and many were taking the risk of repercussions. Many children expressed this fear but were driven to speak up by the feeling that their voice might change something in the end; the world should know and act. By interviewing them, this research hoped to throw light on what was happening beyond the calm security of the typical well-structured research environment: the qualitative equivalent of taking a temperature reading at the surface of a cauldron of molten metal, or measuring the flow at the edge of a river in flood.

The Methodology of Data Collection

The basic way of collecting data was for the researchers to select five (ex) child soldiers and to conduct three interviews with them. The methodology was one of deduction, starting with a general first interview, listening to the tape and going into more detail in the second and then third interview. The interviewers were asked to write up their own impression separately, including some background materials on the countries and children. The researchers were also expected to provide their views on how representative each child was according to their own knowledge.

The South African case study was the first case study conducted with the assistance of a preliminary draft of the Terms of Reference for Case Study researchers. In the light of the comments of the researcher and reactions of assessors of the Case Study report, these Terms of Reference were amended.

The researcher who did the South African case expressed in her notes: "[A]lthough all interviews were taken in English, the language skills of the partner researcher helped T. to describe particular experiences. This was

---

especially the case when the former child soldiers became emotional about certain issues." In a number of case studies the combination of a male and female researcher has proven fruitful as well: "[The] other characteristics of the partner researcher, i.e. male, black, and with a history of (political) activism in the liberation struggle, became important in our encounters and in the development of a relationship of trust with former combatants, [. . .] the fact I was female might have encouraged 'the inner voice' of the former child soldiers rather than the public voice which might have fitted better in a male conversation of armed struggle."[3]

Subsequent case study researchers were provided with a package of five documents that together comprised the Terms of Reference. These were:

1. The Project Proposal
2. Research Guide for Data Collection
3. Researcher Actions and Responsibilities
4. Ethical Guidelines for Researchers
5. Affirmation of Informed Consent for Interviewees

The relevant portion of the Project Proposal summary is quoted at the beginning of this appendix. The full text of the other documents (except for the purely contractual elements of the Researcher Actions and Responsibilities) is reproduced at the end of this appendix to give a clear indication of the methodology used and safeguards adopted. The Researcher Actions and Responsibilities, Ethical Guidelines for Researchers, and Affirmation of Informed Consent were all adapted, with permission, from those that had been used in the separate study of girl soldiers undertaken jointly by the Quaker United Nations Offices in Geneva and New York in 2001.[4]

The Primary Data

As will be seen from the documents reprinted below, the case study reports, transcripts, and tapes of the interviews have been retained by the research directors. For reasons of confidentiality and security, these materials are not public documents and no part of them will be published in full, even when it appeared that individual interviewees would welcome this.

As the text of this book was to be based on selective extracts from the materials in the unpublished case studies, the draft manuscript was sent to all the case study researchers for their review and confirmation that the materials were accurately quoted, reflected their findings without distortion or the omission of any significant points, and to ensure that appropriate acknowledgments were made. A number of amendments were made to take account of the researchers' comments.

Some aggregate information concerning those interviewed for the case studies might nevertheless be useful for readers who wish to locate these findings in a more general context.

The common feature of the 53 informants was that they had, by their own definition, voluntarily joined armed forces or armed groups while still less than 18 years old. Although some were still under 18, and some still serving, at the time of interview, the majority on both counts were not. It was the individual's life history, not current status, that was the criterion for selection, and former rather than current "child soldiers" were in general more accessible for interview. The focus on common features across different contexts meant also that the study was not time-bound; although in fact the research guidelines specified that the respondents ought to be no more than 20 years old, and not to be reporting on involvement that ended more than two years before the date of interview. These restrictions were introduced after the South Africa pilot, and the first restriction was waived in accepting a number of interviews in the other case studies.

Of the 53 respondents, 46 were male and 7 female. With regard to their ages and length of military involvement, the following tabulations are approximate only. It was in the nature of the interviews that precise answers were not always given on specific points; sometimes the answers were of dubious accuracy, and sometimes there were internal inconsistencies.

Age at Time of Interview	Number	
15 and under	4	(from three separate case studies and two continents)
16	7	
17	10	
18	5	
19	8	
20	8	
21 to 29	8	(from three separate case studies and two continents)
30 and over	3	(all from the South Africa pilot study)
Total	53	

Age at Time of First Recruitment	Number	
Less than 10	4	(from case studies in three different continents)
10	5	
11	5	
12	2	
13	6	
14	7	
15	7	
16	13	
17	3	(from case studies in Africa and Asia)
Total	52	(in one instance insufficient information was given)

The interviewees in the South Africa pilot study had been recruited between 1982 and 1990.

Date of First Recruitment	Number
1990/1991	2
1992	2
1993	2
1994	3
1995	2
1996	2
1997	7
1998	9
1999	6
2000	7
2001/2002	5
Total	47

It should be noted that in several cases involvement was not continuous.

Length of Time Between First and Most Recent Involvement	Number	
Less than 1 year	6	(including 1 still apparently active)
1–2 years	5	
2 years	10	(including 3 still apparently active)
3 years	5	(including 3 still apparently active)
4 years	6	(including 1 still apparently active)
5 years	8	(including 5 still apparently active)
6–7 years	4	
8–9 years	6	(including 3 still apparently active)
10 years or more	3	
Total	53	

Analysis and Interpretation of Data

The process of clustering, analyzing, and interpreting the large amount of qualitative research materials from ten highly different situations was one of the major challenges of this book. Several different styles and models have been tried, rejected, and adapted. As this book has a strong comparative spirit and because the samples of children interviewed per country were small and not random, the option of presentation in terms of country cases was not appropriate. In addition, the concerns about the safety of the children precluded using country cases with more contexts, as this could make it easier to trace the children, with all the risks already outlined.

One of the typical features of qualitative research is that we work with "fluid frames," which means that the framing of the phenomenon remains a continuous exercise throughout the research.[5] In this way, fixing the categories is not the means but itself the goal. The contrast with quantitative research is therefore not only an issue of style or tradition, but something that is deeply related to the goal of the research, and therefore with the related approach, methods, and ways of working.[6] Quantitative research can be categorized as looking for the distribution and possible sizing up of phenomena, while qualitative research focuses on the nature of it. It is more concerned with exploring than with verifying. One may note, however, that the inherent rationale of either of the approaches is to enrich an understanding of the problem in hand: the choice of a particular methodology will be dictated by different considerations.

This research project has been very qualitative, not only in means but also in its objective. This is why it cannot systematically explain the direct relationship between the distribution of the variables, nor can it explain how the differences in contexts influence the results. But it can provide insights into the "orientations" of people, and the feelings, thoughts, and ideas that together create a certain "view" that they have on their lives and determines their actions. It is then important to go beyond these orientations as a collection of individual characteristics, and to find a "view" that is, to a certain extent, typical of people in certain situations, a "perspective" that is shared with comparable others—a group perspective.

The majority of the data for this research is collected through open interviewing, for which the analytical model on "view" and "perspective" are helpful. However, most of our researchers (including the authors) were already doing research among the young soldiers, focusing on different questions, and the analysis and reporting was obviously in part informed by insights already gained by other methods.

Every research method has its limits and its strengths. The qualitative research method of open interviewing with a small group of informants from very different cultural contexts places serious limits on the hard conclusions that can be drawn from it. It tends to give the impression that the incomparable are being compared. What are being compared, however, are the reasons young people themselves give for having chosen this path, and the similarities of issues raised from extremely different cultural and economic contexts, which are in themselves interesting enough to present. According to Irving Seidman, the strength of in-depth interviewing of this kind is that "through it we can come to understand the details of people's experience from their point of view. We can see how their individual experience interacts with powerful social and organizational forces that pervade the context in which they live and work."[7]

The "cut and paste" style chosen in this book is the more conventional way of presenting and analyzing interview data, but it has well-known advantages and disadvantages. Excerpts from the transcripts have been organized in categories, within and between which the authors have searched for connecting threads and patterns. One of the advantages of presenting the excerpts thematically in this way is that it reproduces the words of the young soldiers in a direct and striking manner and it makes the reader understand easily the similarities of issues expressed from people that are graphically far from each other. Some critics regard this exercise as an entirely intuitive process.[8] However, the authors did not approach the original transcripts with a set of categories that needed to be filled with excerpts. Rather, by reading through the wealth of data from A to Z, and marking interesting and recurring issues, the categories came up out of the materials and were repeatedly discussed and shared.

The structuring of the interviews has not only been done by the authors, but was an integral part of the interview itself. As only a very broad topic list was provided to the researchers, the process of interpretation and finding connections between the issues has been a constant process. Furthermore, the researchers provided the authors with their interpretations, and commented on and validated the final manuscript. The large group of interns and assistants who have worked on this project have also played a vital role in independently finding key features and linkages and in identifying the critical factors.

This method of data collection and presentation can be criticized for providing too little background, in comparison with alternatives such as "profiling."[9] The authors have, after considerable discussion, decided to provide very limited information on the exact background of the children interviewed in order to reduce the likelihood of their being traced. Their background in terms of such elements as ethnicity, region of origin, religion, age, place in the family, or rural or urban settings were, however, made available by the researchers to the authors. These materials have been used in analyzing, clustering, and interpretating the materials, but will not be made available as such. Although this book might have benefited from more contextual information, the authors do not want the young people who took part in this study to be put at risk for the sake of academic rigor. Furthermore, writing about contexts and history as an outsider is not neutral, nor is it necessarily in line with the way the young people themselves see and interpret their surroundings. It might even suggest linkages between context and reasons for joining, which are perceived differently by those interviewed. For the purpose of this book, the authors have chosen to retain its "emic"[10] spirit. The material is sufficiently rich and informative to deepen the understanding of the phenomenon of children participating in armed conflict, such that only a minimum of contextual information is necessary (see Annex II and, to some extent, Chapter 1).

It is important to stress that none of the samples were large enough to throw any effective light on the individual conflict situations, or to permit valid comparisons between regions or between the experiences of young people attached to different kinds of armed forces or armed groups. It is only from the testimony of the 53 taken together, and recognizing their diverse cultural contexts, that some insight can be gained into the unique shared aspect of their experience: that they all, before adulthood, chose to become associated with armed forces or groups. The only systematic comparisons made between subsets of the interviewees is in the chapter on girls and boys, for which purpose it was possible to enlarge the sample of girls by drawing, with permission, on materials from two completely separate recent research projects. Although the authors recognize that the sample has been thin and widespread, this annex has explained the numerous safeguards established in order to make such a comparison valid.

Instructions Provided to Researchers

Research Guide for Data Collection

The research guide printed below has been specially developed for this project by one of the authors, and researchers were explicitly asked to do their work on that basis.

Contents: A. Selection of Participants and Security
             B. Guiding Principles for the Interviews
             C. Topics for the Open Interviews
             D. Outputs and Reporting

A. Selection of Participants and Security

In the light of the strictly qualitative research methodology chosen, you have a rather large freedom to select your participants, who should be under 18 years old (or between 18 and 20 telling their stories about the period before they were 18). In order to choose your participants you should build if possible onto research you are already undertaking, using the contacts you have already. The most important guiding principle is that you have established a relationship of confidence. As the young people of our target group often have a very sensitive social status, mutual trust and willingness to tell their stories is key.

Within this framework, and other things being equal, you should select your respondents with a view to achieving as wide a mix as possible on the following criteria:

- Male and female
- Those still serving, those who were officially demobilized, and those who "auto-demobilized"
- Those who fight/fought with government forces, with armed opposition groups, and armed groups not opposing the government
- Those with frontline experience and those who have performed exclusively support roles
- Those from urban and rural backgrounds
- Members of as many different ethnic and religious communities as possible

Try as much as possible to get clearance for the interview from adults or organizations that have the prime responsibility over the young soldier. If you are interviewing soldiers that are still part of an armed group, you might want to get clearance from the leader right above him (do not go up too high in the hierarchy as this might create more waves than necessary).

Try to be aware of local politics and power games among soldiers, ethnic groups, etc. Some young soldiers might be too eager to talk to you because they see in you a way to gain power or status. These things you will have to play by ear, and this is why we prefer research assistants who are already working in the field.

B. Guiding Principles for the Interviews[11]

Listen more, talk less. Listening is the most important skill in interviewing. The hardest work for most interviewers is to keep quiet and to listen actively.

Interviewers must listen on at least three levels. First, they must listen to what the participant is saying. They must concentrate on the substance to make sure that they understand it and to assess whether what they are hearing is as detailed and complete as they would like it to be. They must concentrate so that they internalize what participants say. Later, interviewers' questions will often flow from this earlier listening.

On the second level, interviewers must listen for what we call "inner voice," as opposed to an outer, more public voice. An outer, or public, voice always reflects an awareness of the audience. It is not untrue; it is guarded. It is a voice that participants would use if they were talking to an audience of 300 in an auditorium.

There is a language of the outer voice to which interviewers can become sensitive. For example, whenever we hear participants talk about the problems they are facing as a "challenge" or their work as an "adventure," I sense that I am hearing a public voice, and we search for ways to get the inner voice. *Challenge* and *adventure* convey the positive aspects of a participant's grappling with a difficult experience, but not the struggle. Another word that attracts our attention is *fascinate*. I often hear that word on talk-show interviews; it usually works to communicate some sort of interest while covering up the exact nature of the interest. By taking participants' language seriously without making them feel defensive about it, interviewers can encourage a level of thoughtfulness more characteristic of inner voice.

On a third level, interviewers must listen while remaining aware of the process as well as the substance. They must be sensitive to the participant's energy level and any nonverbal cues he or she may be offering. Interviewers must listen hard to assess the progress of the interview and to stay alert for cues about how to move the interview forward as necessary.

This type of active listening concentration and focus goes beyond what we usually do in everyday life. It requires that, for a good part of the time, we quash our normal instinct to talk. At the same time, interviewers must be ready to say something when a navigational nudge is needed.

In order to facilitate active listening, in addition to tape-recording the interview, interviewers can take notes. These working notes help interviewers concentrate on what the participant is saying. They also help to keep interviewers from interrupting the participant by allowing them to keep track of things that the participant has mentioned in order to come back to these subjects when the timing is right.

A good way to gauge listening skills is to transcribe an interview tape. Separate the interviewers' questions from the participant's responses by new paragraphs. Compare the relative length of the participant's paragraphs with the interviewer's. If the interviewer is listening well, his or her paragraphs will be short and relatively infrequently interspersed among the longer paragraphs of the participant's responses.

Follow up on what the participant says. When interviewers do talk in an interview, they usually ask questions. The key to asking questions during in-depth interviewing is to let them follow, as much as possible, from what the participant is saying. Although the interviewer comes to each interview with a basic question that establishes the purpose and focus of the interview, it is in response to what the participant says that the interviewer follows up, asks for clarification, seeks concrete details, and requests stories. Rather than preparing a preset interview guide, the interviewer's basic work in this approach to interviewing is to listen actively and to move the interview forward as much as possible by building on what the participant has begun to share.

Ask questions when you do not understand. It is hard work to understand everything people say. Sometimes the context is not clear. At other times we do not understand the specific reference of what someone is saying. In everyday conversation we often let such things slide by without understanding them. In interviewing, such sliding undermines the process.

The interview structure is cumulative. One interview establishes the context for the next. Not having understood something in an early interview, an interviewer might miss the significance of something a participant says later. Passages in interviews become links to each other in ways that cannot be foretold. Also, the interviewer who lets a participant know when he or she does not understand something shows the person that the interviewer is listening.

Sometimes it is difficult to get the chronology of an experience straight. It is important for interviewers to understand experiences in the context of time. A question like, "Can you tell me again when that happened?" is a reasonable one. We use the word *again* so as not to imply to participants that they are not being clear, thereby making them defensive, but rather, as is often the case, to suggest that we were not just attentive enough the first time around.

Sometimes participants use vague words that seem to be communicating but are not explicit.

Avoid leading questions (ask open-ended questions). A leading question is one that influences the direction the response will take. Sometimes the lead is in the intonation of the question: the tone implies an expectation. Sometimes it is in the wording, syntax, and intonation of the question, as when an interviewer asks, "Did you *really* mean to do that?" Sometimes the lead is in the conclusion implied by the question.

An open-ended question, unlike a leading question, establishes the territory to be explored while allowing the participant to take any direction he or she wants. It does not presume the answer. There are at least two types of open-ended questions especially relevant to in-depth interviewing. One is the "grand tour" question, in which the interviewer asks the participant to reconstruct a significant segment of an experience.

There is also the "mini tour" in which the interviewer asks the participant to reconstruct the details of a more limited time span or of a particular experience.

A second type of open-ended question focuses more on the subjective experience of the participant than on the external structure. For example, a participant might begin to talk about her experience in the army. After asking her what happened during the battle, the interviewer might ask her to talk about what that battle was like for her.

Although there are many approaches to open-ended questioning, when we are interested in understanding the participant's subjective experience, we often find ourselves asking the question, "What was that like for you?" It is not possible to experience what the participant experienced—if we could, then we would be the participants. Perhaps the closest we can come is to ask the metaphorical question implied in the word *like*. When interviewers ask what something was like for participants, they are giving them the chance to reconstruct their experience *according to their own sense of what was important,* unguided by the interviewer.

Follow up, don't interrupt. Avoid interrupting participants when they are talking. Often an interviewer is more interested in something a participant says than the speaker seems to be. While the participant continues talking, the interviewer feels strongly tempted to interrupt to pursue the interesting point. Rather than doing so, however, the interviewer can jot down the key word and follow up on it later, when doing so will not interrupt the participant's train of thought. The opportunity may come later in the same interview or even in a subsequent one.

Tolerate silence. Interviewers sometimes get impatient and uncomfortable with silence. They project that discomfort onto their participants. They see pauses as voids and jump into the interview with a quick question to fill the void. A useful exercise is to play back an interview tape and record how much time the interviewer gives the participant to think before he or she jumps in with a question. The new interviewers think they are waiting a considerable time before asking their next question, but when we go over audiotapes of their interviews, we determine that in reality they are waiting only a second or two. Thoughtfulness takes time; if interviewers can learn to tolerate either the silence that sometimes follows a question or a pause within a participant's reconstruction, they may hear things they would never have heard if they had leapt in with another question to break the silence.

As in other aspects of interviewing, there is a delicate balance between jumping in too soon with a question and waiting too long in silence. There are no rules of thumb here. It is important to give your participant space to think, reflect, and add to what he or she has said. This may take a second or two for some participants and twenty seconds for others.

Linguistic differences. An issue embedded in many of the social relationships described above is linguistic differences between interviewers and participants. Sometimes English-speaking researchers interview participants for whom English is not their first language. If interviewers are fluent in the participants' mother tongue and interview in that language, they will subsequently face the complexity of translation. The issue of finding the right word in English or any other language to represent the full sense of the word the participants spoke in their native language is demanding and requires a great deal of care.

What is at issue in interviewing participants whose first language is not that of the interviewer is the extent to which the language used by both the participants and the interviewer affects the progress of the interview. The thinking of both the participants and the interviewer is intertwined with the language they are using. As in most issues regarding interviewing, there is not one right way to respond to these situations, except to recognize the importance of language and culture to thought. With that awareness, both interviewer and participants can experiment with ways of talking to each other that most authentically reflect their thinking.

If the participant and the interviewer do not have a shared language of reasonable understanding the interviewer should recruit a translator. The translator should read and understand this briefing note and the overall objective of the research and the interview. You ask questions in English/French and the translator asks questions in the local language. Only once in a while the translator says in a few words to you what they are talking about. You can just make limited suggestions to the translator who largely replaces you in guiding the process of the interview. Make sure you train him well in avoiding leading questions, etc. You will transcribe the tapes together, discuss your findings, and prepare a topic list for the next interview which will flow from the findings and gaps in the first session. Please discuss with us before recruiting a translator. In such a case, the translator will also need to sign the "Ethical Guidelines for Interviewers."

Avoid a therapeutic relationship. Interviewers must avoid changing the interviewing relationship into a therapeutic one. It is essential that research interviewers not confuse themselves with therapists. The goals are different. The researcher is there to learn, not to treat the participant. The participant did not seek out the researcher and is not a patient. The researcher will see the participant a few times, after which their connection will substantially end. They will not have a continuing relationship in which the researcher takes some measure of ongoing responsibility. Researchers are unlikely to be trained therapists. They should know both their own limits and those imposed by the structure and goal of the interviewing process. Researchers must be very cautious about suggesting solutions for problems in areas of participants' private lives and personal complexities to which they are ill-equipped to respond and for which they can take no effective responsibility.

But even when researchers exercise such caution, the intimacy that can develop in in-depth interviewing sometimes threatens those limits, and a participant may find the interviewing process emotionally troubling. Participants may start to cry in an interview. Interviewers may themselves become upset in the face of a participant's tears and not know what to do. Let the participant work out the distress without interfering and taking inappropriate responsibility for it. On the other hand, if the distress continues, the interviewer then has the responsibility to pull back from whatever is causing it.

The key to negotiating potentially troubled waters is to assess how much responsibility the interviewer can effectively take in navigating them.

Before the second session, you might want to consult adults surrounding him/her and seek their advice or ask their assistance on psychological aftercare, without telling any details of things said to you in confidence.

Reciprocity. The issue of reciprocity in the interviewing relationship can be troubling. The more the interviewing relationship is charged with issues of race, ethnicity, class, and gender, the more complicated the problem of reciprocity can be. This is the most problematic aspect of interviewing—being sympathetic to the argument that the researcher gets more out of the process than the participant.

The reciprocity that can be offered in an interview is that which flows from the interest in the participant's experience, and honoring their words when we present their experience to a larger public. Although at the conclusion of the interview you might present participants with a small gift, that gift is only a token of appreciation in the fullest sense of the word *token*: to say thank you and to mark the conclusion of that part of our interviewing relationship. You are encouraged to provide drinks and food during or after the interview, if appropriate.

C. Topic List for the Open Interviews

The open and unstructured interviews should cover the following topics and elicit the information indicated. Respondents should not be discouraged if they wish to speak at length about their experiences while soldiers or about their present situation and prospects, but the interviewer must remain aware that these are not the primary focus of the current project, and must ensure that somehow all the core topics are covered and that the respondent is encouraged to go into detail on these.

    a. Background of the participant (age, region of origin, religion, ethnic group, level of education, physical condition, profession of his/her parents).

    b. What were they doing before the war/before joining the war (school, work, housing, friends, ideals, ideas on the future, well or badly off, etc)?

    c. How did they become aware of the conflict? Do they remember a time before it started? What happened to them when it started? How did they feel about it?

d. When and how did they become aware of the possibility of joining the conflict?

e. Why did they decide to join? What would have happened to them if they had not joined? Did their friends join or not? Do they know what happened to those who did not?

f. When and how did they join? Specific reasons. What triggered them to join?

g. What was their career as a soldier? Which party to the conflict did they join? How long did they serve? What (if not too revealing) is/was their rank? Are they now demobilized?

h. What did they like about being a soldier? What did they dislike about being a soldier?

i. Why and how did they stop being a soldier/combatant? (Or if still enrolled why had they decided not to stop?)

j. What is their present situation? What do they like/dislike about no longer being a soldier? Would anything have made the transition easier? Would they have any advice for young persons currently contemplating enlisting?

k. How do they see their future? (This is not the data we are concentrating on, so it should be kept brief. It is mainly to bring the interview to a close and the participant back to the future with his/her (maybe painful) thoughts.)

The first interview should cover all topics. Then the researcher should listen to the tapes and come back for a second interview on specific topics that need deepening. Employ the same procedure for the third interview. You must undertake in-depth interviews.

D. Outputs and Reporting

The outputs from each case study researcher will be:

Output 1. Tapes. Interviews will be taped (unless the respondent does not permit this); anonymity will be assured (e.g., names will not be recorded and will not be used to label the tapes).

Output 2. Transcripts. The full text of the interviews must be transcribed onto a diskette. If interviews are taken in the local language, the local language should be transcribed and then translated into English. An "Affirmation of Informed Consent" form should be "signed" by each interviewee.

Output 3. Photographs. Interviewers are encouraged to take or collect photographs. However, no picture should be taken or provided by the interviewee as this might threaten his/her security; furthermore, this might not be acceptable in the cultural setting. Other organizations in the country can be contacted for appropriate photographs. The United Nations connection of the project should be explained in this case.

It would be highly appreciated if the interviewee was willing to do one or two drawings illustrating why they joined, and which might also provide a focus for a subsequent interview.

(Be prepared to provide them with paper and crayons).

Output 4. Reports. In order to better analyze and place the interviews, the researcher is asked to provide:

- A two/three-page background paper on the context of the interview. In this you can express your own feelings and impressions of the interview, the setting, the cultural context, if you think the person was free to talk, how honest he or she was, and if this was a unique case or that there are many children like him or her.
- A one/two-page description of the national situation and the local situation (social, cultural, economic, religious, security, etc.) in relation to that child.

A complete package of outputs, that is, tape, transcript, "Affirmation of Informed Consent" form, translation (if necessary), context report, background analyses, and, if obtained, illustrative materials (photographs and/or sketches) should be submitted for each interviewee. Text outputs (i.e., all except tapes and illustrative materials) should be submitted first by e-mail, followed by diskettes accompanied by hard copy.

The researcher responsible for each case study will also have submitted separately the following signed forms (as well as retaining a copy for reference):

- Interviewer actions and responsibilities signed by him/herself
- Ethical guidelines for researchers signed separately by all persons having access to any of the interview material

Researcher Actions and Responsibilities

At all times, the safety and security of the interviewee and others involved in this project is more important than the data.

As a researcher for the Voices of Young Soldiers Project, my signature on this document confirms my acceptance of the following actions and responsibilities.

I attach a signed copy of the Ethical Guidelines for Researchers, which I have read and carefully noted and which I agree to abide by.

[*Contractual details omitted*]

1. Identify and interview between five and seven current or former soldiers/combatants between the ages of 10 and 20 years who were recruited under the age of 18 and have not been out of the armed force or group for more than two years.
2. Conduct interviews only when assured that the interviewee understands the entire process outlined in the Interviewee Informed Consent Form and has signed the form (the use of an alias is acceptable).
3. Arrange times, places, and length of meetings keeping safety, confidentiality, privacy, and convenience in mind. Follow the in-depth interview method as outlined in the "Research Guide."
4. Subject to the consent of the interviewee, make a tape recording of the interview, and transcribe it, omitting only identifying names.
5. Take notes in addition to recording.
6. If the interviewee is not prepared to allow the interviews to be recorded, use notes to make as complete and accurate a written transcript of the interview as is possible but omitting identifying names.
7. Transcribe (and if necessary translate) the interview verbatim without making changes in the words, but append clarifications and explanations of cultural context where necessary, in dialogue, where relevant, with the local assistant.
8. Erase from the tapes any accidental naming of any interviewee or contact person or other direct means of identifying the interviewee (e.g., precise date of birth, full name of relative) but otherwise do not amend the taped record in any way.
9. Submit or read each transcript to the interviewee (preferably at the beginning of the next interview) for any suggested amendments or clarifications.
10. In accordance with the "Ethical Guidelines for Researchers," treat the identity of interviewees and contacts and all the material revealed in the interviews in the strictest confidence; do not grant anyone access to this information unless this is essential,

e.g., for purposes of translation, and then only with the advance consent of the project management and after obtaining that person's signature on a copy of the "Ethical Guidelines for Researchers."

[Technical instructions for submission of materials and form for signature omitted]

Ethical Guidelines for Researchers

I *[name]* agree as a Researcher in the Voices of Young Soldiers Research Project to abide by the following guidelines:

1. Follow the process for contacting and interviewing as outlined in our Terms of Reference and Research Guide.
2. Keep all names and information confidential. Never use any identifying names in the written and recorded material.
3. Give priority to protecting the safety, security, and privacy of the interviewee at all times.
4. Read through the "Informed Consent" form with each interviewee, satisfy myself that it is understood, and obtain the signature (alias acceptable) of the interviewee prior to any interview taking place.
5. Remain sensitive to the interviewee and stop the interviewing if this appears necessary or is requested by the interviewee.
6. Not to raise expectations or make promises that cannot be fulfilled.
7. Honor all commitments made to the interviewee as outlined in the "Interviewee Informed Consent" form.
8. Report the data with as much accuracy as possible and honor the voice, i.e., the story as given by the interviewee, subject only to changes to preserve confidentiality.
9. Report promptly to the project management any difficulties, problems, or inadvertent breaches of these guidelines which might impinge upon the security of anyone involved.

I certify that I have read and understood the above "Ethical Guidelines for Researchers" and agree to act in accordance with them. I have retained a copy for my own reference.

Signature _____ Date _____

Affirmation of Informed Consent for Interviewee

[This consent form will be reviewed verbally with the interviewee to be certain that it is understood. Once understood, the written consent form is presented for signature. Research interviews may not be conducted before this has taken place.]

I am _____ and I am working with the Voices of Young Soldiers Project. I am interested in understanding the story of your life. What kinds of things you did when you were younger, where you lived, who you lived with, what you liked to do, who you enjoyed being with, and other information about your family and community that you remember and would like to share with me. I would also like to hear about why and how you became a soldier. I would be interested in knowing what happened to you when you were a soldier. I am also interested in hearing about your life as it is now—the way it is today and how you see the future.

What you and other young people tell us will be used to assist groups like ours to begin to plan programs that will include what young people like yourself tell us you need. It would help us to know the kinds of things that would be most helpful for you to have a better and easier life. The experiences you have had in your life will help us to understand what we need to do for the young people who have been soldiers. A report will be written at the end, combining stories of all the young soldiers we talk to from different countries. All of this information will help us to know what the young soldiers want and need as they continue to build their life.

If you give me permission I would like to tape record what you tell me. I can also just write what you tell me. You can decide if you would like me to use the tape recorder or write what you tell me. After we have finished, if you like, you and I can read together the story you have told me. If you want to make any changes in what I have written you can tell me when we go over your story.

When I am writing I will not use your name or anyone's real name. If we are using the tape recorder, you can use different names for people so that the person's real name will be private and protected.

I will ask you to meet with me at least three different times. Each time we would meet for about 1½ hours. We will agree on a time and place that is comfortable, private, and safe. A second interviewer may be with me to be sure I am recording your story just the way you are telling it to me.

One other thing that is very important for you to know: if you change your mind, for whatever reason, and decide you do not want to continue talking with me, we will stop. You should not feel bad about doing this because everyone has the right to change their mind and make their own personal decisions. You can make that decision at anytime, during any of the interviews.

I have reviewed this information and I agree to participate in this study.

Signature _____ Date _____

Notes

1. The interviewees from Pakistan and Afghanistan were in both cases fighting in Afghanistan, and in the case of the United Kingdom—where interviewees came from both mainland Britain and from Northern Ireland—one of the soldiers from the British Army served in Northern Ireland.

2. Coalition to Stop the Use of Child Soldiers 2001.

3. Beirens 2002.

4. The authors are particularly grateful to Dr. Yvonne E. Keairns, chief researcher on the girl soldiers project, for access to and permission to use these materials. The results were published under the title of *Voices of Girl Child Soldiers: Summary Report* (Keairns 2002): the title was chosen completely independently of the present project.

5. Ragin 1994, pp. 75–76.

6. This paragraph is inspired by the internet article of Paul ten Have, "Probleemstelling in Kwalitatief Sociologisch Onderzoek": www2.fmg.uva.nl/emac/PS.htm.

7. Seidman 1998, p. 112.

8. Ibid., p. 109, citing Tagg 1985.

9. This method was developed by Studs Terkel in *Working* (1972).

10. The *emic* perspective in ethnography uses the concepts and categories that are relevant and meaningful to the culture under analysis.

11. Most of the data for this section comes from Seidman 1998.

APPENDIX 2

Conflict Profiles

AFGHANISTAN

Population (2003): 24 million (UN)

Secondary school enrollment 2000–2001: No figures available

Percentage of population aged 15–24 who are illiterate:
No figures available

Life expectancy: 43 years (men), 43 years (women) (UN)

Average annual income: No figures available

Capital: Kabul

Afghanistan's recent history is characterized by war and civil unrest.
The country suffers from enormous poverty, a crumbling infrastructure,
and widespread land mines.

The Soviet Union invaded Afghanistan in 1979 but was forced to
withdraw 10 years later by anti-Communist Mojahedin forces supplied
and trained by the United States, Saudi Arabia, Pakistan, and others.
The Mojahedin proved incapable of unity following the departure of the
Soviets, however, and violent fighting broke out between rival factions.
The head of state, Najibullah, lost effective control of the country in
1990 and ceased to be president. After a period of major instability and
anarchy, which involved two attacks on Kabul in 1993 and 1994 in
which up to 10,000 persons died on each occasion, the fundamentalist
Islamic Taliban gained total control of the country in 1996.

The Taliban, led by Mullah Omar, succeeded in bringing stability to
Afghanistan. The Taliban made an arrangement with Pakistani authorities, its main supporter during this period, that resulted in commercial

development being conducted largely through Pakistan and its resources. Life under Taliban rule meant that such things as girls' schools and centuries-old historic religous statues and artwork were destroyed. A series of extreme laws were introduced that banned the possession of such things as chess sets, televisions, playing cards, neckties, and wigs. Women, allowed some liberation and education under the Najibullah regime, were forced to wear burkhas (dark, all-covering clothes). Men were required to wear full beards. Penalties for breaching these laws were harsh, and included prison and violent beatings.

The Taliban were ousted by a coalition led by the United States in November 2001, after refusing to turn over Osama bin Laden and members of his Al Qaeda terrorist network. Many Taliban leaders, including Mullah Omar, fled Afghanistan and are now in hiding. An interim government, with the purpose of rebuilding the country, was established. In June 2002, Hamid Karzai was elected as the official head of state for the transitional administration.

COLOMBIA

Population (2001): 42.8 million, of whom 16.4 million are under 18 (UNICEF)

Secondary school enrollment 2000–2001: 70 percent (gross) or 57 percent (net) (UNESCO)

Percentage of population aged 15–24 who are illiterate: 3.1 percent (UNESCO)

Life expectancy: 69 years (men), 75 years (women) (UN)

Average annual income (2001): US$1,890 (World Bank)

Capital: Bogota

Colombia is a country of significant natural resources and a diverse culture reflecting the indigenous Indian, Spanish, and African origins of its people. It enjoys a long tradition of elected civilian governments. However, Colombia has a highly stratified society where the traditionally rich families of Spanish descent have benefited from the wealth of the country to a far greater degree than the majority of the population, who are mostly of mixed race. Colombia has become a byword for drug cartels, violence, guerrilla insurgencies, and gross human rights violations.

In the mid-1960s two main guerrilla groups, the Revolutionary Armed Forces of Colombia (FARC) and National Liberation Army (ELN), were established. Between 1978 and 1982, the government focused on ending the limited but persistent insurgencies from these groups. In 1984, President Belisario Betancur negotiated a cease-fire that included the release of many guerrillas imprisoned during the effort to overpower the insurgents. The cease-fire ended when Democratic Alliance/M-19 (AD/M-19) guerrillas resumed fighting in 1985. An attack on the Palace of Justice in Bogota by this group followed in November 1985. Although the government and the FARC renewed their truce in March 1986, peace with other revolutionary movements, in particular the AD/M-19, then the largest insurgent group, and the ELN did not materialize. The AD/M-19 and several smaller guerrilla groups were successfully incorporated into a peace process during the late 1980s. The FARC had declared a unilateral cease-fire under Betancur, which led to the establishment of the Patriotic Union Party (UP) political organization. After growing violence against its UP members, the truce with the FARC ended in 1990.

Following administrations have had to contend with the guerrillas, right-wing paramilitary groups who are sometimes in the pay of drug traffickers and large landowners and backed by elements in the army and the police, and narcotics traffickers. Early initiatives in the Colombian peace process initiated under President Pastrana in 1998 gave reason for some optimism, though the growing severity of countrywide guerrilla attacks by the FARC and ELN, and smaller movements, as well as the growth of drug production and the spread of paramilitary groups, has made it difficult to solve the country's problems. After more than three years of talks, President Pastrana suspended the peace process with the FARC on 21 February 2002. The government and ELN, after suspending talks in 2001, have resumed discussions aimed at opening a formal peace process.

While no single explanation fully addresses the deep roots of Colombia's present-day troubles, they include limited government presence in large areas of the interior, the expansion of illicit drug cultivation, endemic violence, and social inequities.

REPUBLIC OF CONGO (CONGO-BRAZZAVILLE)

Population (2001): 3.1 million of whom 1.6 million are under 18 (UNICEF)

Secondary school enrollment 2000–2001: 42 percent (gross, no net figures available) (UNESCO)

Percentage of population aged 15–24 who are illiterate: 2.6 percent (UNESCO)

Life expectancy: 47 years (men), 50 years (women) (UN)

Average annual income (2001): US$640 (World Bank)

Capital: Brazzaville

Congo gained its independence from France in 1960. After three relatively peaceful but coup-ridden decades, the country experienced two destructive bouts of fighting.

In 1993, disputed parliamentary elections led to bloody, ethnically-based fighting between armed opposition supporters and the government military. The "Zulu" militia backed Lissouba, the "Ninja" militia supported Kolélas, and the "Cobras" supported Sassou-Nguesso. Hundreds were killed and the three militias remained in conflict until January 1995, when a new cross-party alliance under Brigadier General Jacques Joachim Yhombi-Opango assumed power. The militias signed a peace accord in December 1995, although the conditions of the agreement were never met.

In 1997, despite the efforts of the African Union, the United Nations, and regional mediators, ethnic and political tensions led to full-scale civil war. Fighting was centered in Brazzaville, which was split into three zones occupied by the militias of the three leading players. Five thousand foreign nationals were evacuated from Brazzaville by the French army. Seven hundred thousand people fled Brazzaville, spreading throughout the country and to the Democratic Republic of Congo. In August, President Lissouba appointed Kolélas as prime minister, leading to gains for the combined militias. In October, Angolan troops entered Congo to support Sassou-Nguesso. This altered the balance of power in Sassou-Nguesso's favor. He proclaimed himself president on 25 October 1997, and Lissouba and Kolélas fled the country.

President Sassou-Nguesso formed a "Government of National Unity" composed mainly of his supporters. In December 1998, fighting and looting broke out once again, in the Pool region of Brazzaville. Sassou-Nguesso claimed that it was an attempted coup by militias loyal to

Lissouba and Kolélas, but there were widespread reports of looting and killing of civilians by government troops and armed militias. Hundreds of thousands of civilians were again displaced from Brazzaville. Peace agreements were signed in November and December 1999 by the government forces and all major rebel militias in Congo-Brazzaville.

More than 630,000 of the 810,000 people displaced by the war have now returned, and malnutrition and death rates have dropped. The vital railway line between Brazzaville and Pointe-Noire has reopened and the security situation is slowly improving. In March 2003, the Ninja rebels signed a new commitment to peace with the government, and have begun disarmament and reintegration into wider society.

DEMOCRATIC REPUBLIC OF CONGO (DRC)

Population (2001): 52.5 million of whom 29 million are under 18 (UNICEF)

Secondary school enrollment 2000–2001: 18 percent (gross) or 12 percent (net) (UNESCO)

Percentage of population aged 15–24 who are illiterate: 18.3 percent (UNESCO)

Life expectancy: 41 years (men), 43 years (women) (UN)

Average annual income (2001): US$80 (World Bank)

Capital: Kinshasa

The Democratic Republic of Congo (DRC) gained its independence from Belgium in 1960. Recently, this vast country with immense economic resources has been at the center of what some have called Africa's worst war. Human rights organizations estimate that 2.5 million people have been killed, either as a direct result of fighting or because of disease and malnutrition, since the conflict began in August 1998.

After the 1994 Rwanda genocide, President Mobutu (leader since seizing power in 1965) gave sanctuary and support to Hutu refugees, members of the former Rwandan Government Army (FAR). This exacerbated long-standing ethnic tensions with Tutsi inhabitants (Banyamulenge) in the east of the DRC (at the time known as Zaire). In October 1996, the Banyamulenge, led by Laurent Kabila, and other rebel groups formed the Alliance of Democratic Forces for the Liberation of Congo-Zaire (AFDL) and rose in revolt. The AFDL made dramatic gains against the demoralized government army, the Zairian Armed Forces (FAZ). The rebels entered Kinshasa on 17 May and Kabila declared himself president. Mobutu fled to Morocco where he subsequently died.

Over the next year, relations between Kabila and his foreign backers deteriorated. In July 1998, Kabila ordered all foreign troops to leave. Most refused to leave and in August fighting erupted throughout the country as Rwandan troops in the DRC "mutinied" and fresh Rwandan and Ugandan troops entered the DRC. Rwandan troops flew to Bas-Congo with the intention of marching on Kinshasa, ousting Laurent Kabila, and replacing him with the newly formed Rwandan-backed rebel group called the Congolese Rally for Democracy (RCD). The Rwandan campaign was thwarted at the last minute when Angolan, Zimbabwean, and Namibian troops intervened on behalf of the DRC government. The Rwandans and the RCD withdrew to eastern DRC, where they established de facto control over portions of the region and continued to fight the Congolese army and its foreign allies. In February 1999, Uganda backed the formation of a rebel group called the Movement for the Liberation of Congo (MLC), which drew support from among ex-Mobutuists and ex-FAZ soldiers in Equateur province (Mobutu's home province). Together, Uganda and the MLC established control over the northern third of the DRC. By this stage, the DRC was effectively divided into three segments, and the parties controlling each segment had reached military deadlock. In July 1999, a cease-fire was proposed in Lusaka, Zambia, which all parties signed by the end of August.

On 16 January 2001, Laurent Kabila was assassinated. His son, Joseph Kabila, was sworn in as the new president on 26 January. He has undertaken to implement the Lusaka agreement, open up internal politics, improve human rights, and liberalize the economy.

NORTHERN IRELAND

Population: 1.7 million of whom 0.45 million are under 18 (Northern Ireland Statistics website: www.nisra.gov.uk)[1]

Secondary school enrollment 2000–2001: 89.6 percent (net, no gross figures available) (Department of Education, Northern Ireland)

Percentage of population aged 15–24 who are illiterate: No figures are available

Life expectancy: 75 years (men), 80 years (women) (Northern Ireland Statistics website: www.nisra.gov.uk)

Average annual income (2000): US$30,700 (Northern Ireland Statistics and Research Agency)

Capital: Belfast

The origins of the opposition between the cultural and political traditions of Catholic and Protestant in Northern Ireland can be said to be found in the early seventeenth century, when Protestants from Britain were encouraged to settle in Ulster, the northernmost province of Ireland, on land previously owned by the indigenous Catholic nobility. This colonization sowed the seeds of distrust, resentment, and conflict that were to mark relations for the next three centuries.

By the beginning of the 20th century, while the majority of the Catholic population in Ireland wished for independence from Britain, the majority of the Protestants of Ulster were concerned that an independent united Ireland would leave them dominated by Catholics. The partition of Ireland was a compromise between these two positions. Twenty-six counties formed the almost exclusively Catholic "Irish Free State" (later the Republic of Ireland), and six made up the predominantly Protestant "Northern Ireland," an autonomous region of the United Kingdom. From 1921 to 1972, Northern Ireland had its own regional government and parliament based in Belfast. However, since the political parties were divided along ethnic and religious lines, there was a permanent Protestant majority in the Northern Ireland parliament and hence in its government.

The present unrest began in 1968 after the emergence of a civil rights movement campaigning against discrimination against Catholics by successive Northern Ireland governments. Attempts to suppress the movement helped to rejuvenate militant republicanism in the form of the Provisional Irish Republican Army (IRA). Support for the openly violent IRA increased rapidly, while militant Loyalist attacks on Catholic civilians became more frequent. In 1969 the regular army was deployed in an attempt to restore order. The political structure progressively fragmented and the violence worsened, leading, after a series of particularly brutal incidents involving the IRA, Loyalist terrorists, and indeed the British army itself, to the suspension of the Northern Ireland government and the beginning of direct rule from London in 1972.

Meanwhile, the intercommunal rioting of the late 1960s was gradually replaced by a more complex and violent conflict. The protagonists were the British government, represented by its army, locally recruited regiments, and a militarized police force; Republican paramilitaries, mainly the IRA, but also smaller violent groups such as the Irish National Liberation Army (INLA); and Loyalist paramilitaries, the Ulster Defence Association/Ulster Freedom Fighters (UDA/UDF), and the Ulster Volunteer Force (UVF). By the mid-1990s more than 3,500 people had been killed during what is colloquially known as "the Troubles."

Between 1972 and 1998, several initiatives were developed by successive British governments, increasingly with the involvement of the Irish Republic, aimed at finding a solution to the conflict and reestablishing a system of government that would be stable and fair to both communities. The ebb and flow of discussion and negotiation continued into the 1990s, during which years the U.S. government began to provide support and pressure for the peace process.

An IRA cease-fire and nearly two years of multiparty negotiations resulted in the Good Friday Agreement of 10 April 1998. Key elements of the agreement included devolved government, a commitment of the parties to work toward "total disarmament of all paramilitary organizations," police reform, and enhanced mechanisms to guarantee human rights and equal opportunity, as well as arrangements to increase and strengthen relationships between the governments of Northern Ireland and the Irish Republic. A directly elected assembly and an executive were established and functioned until October 2002. Loss of trust on both sides of the community and an increase in violence led to political paralysis within the assembly and executive. On 14 October, the devolved government was suspended once again. Although a number of institutions established through the Good Friday Agreement continue to function and the peace process is not dead, by October 2003 negotiations had not succeeded in reestablishing a devolved government.

SIERRA LEONE

Population (2001): 4.6 million of whom 2.3 million are under 18 (UNICEF)

Secondary school enrollment 2000–2001: 26 percent (gross) and 26 percent (net) (UNESCO)

Percentage of population aged 15–24 who are illiterate: Figures not available (UNESCO)

Life expectancy: 33 years (men), 35 years (women) (UN)

Average annual income (2001): US$140 (World Bank)

Capital: Freetown

The West African state of Sierra Leone gained its independence from the United Kingdom in 1961. In the following 30 years, though rich in diamonds and nominally a democratic republic, the country rarely experienced stability as economic mismanagement and corruption marginalized the majority who live in the provinces in favor of a Freetown elite. In 1991, civil war erupted.

Brigadier General Joseph Momoh, president since 1985, had failed to reverse economic decline. In April 1991, the Revolutionary United Front (RUF), led by former army corporal Foday Sankoh and supported by President Charles Taylor of Liberia, invaded Sierra Leone. Momoh was powerless to deal with the insurgents and was overthrown in a military coup in 1992. Captain Valentine Strasser was installed as head of the National Provincial Ruling Council (NPRC). He promised to rid the country of corruption and defeat the RUF, but failed. He was, in turn, overthrown by Captain Julius Maada Bio in early 1996. Under pressure from civil society, Bio called multiparty elections in February 1996, and Ahmad Tejan Kabbah of the Sierra Leone People's Party (SLPP) won the presidency.

On 25 May 1997, disaffected soldiers staged a military coup and called on Major Johnny Paul Koroma, in prison on treason charges, to be their leader. Koroma formed the Armed Forces Revolutionary Council (AFRC) and, in an effort to halt the war, invited the RUF to join him. The military junta failed to attract international support and was removed by the Nigerian-led Economic Community of West African States Monitoring Group (ECOMOG) and the Sierra Leone Civil Defense Forces (CDF) from Freetown in February 1998. In March, Kabbah made a triumphant return to Freetown amid scenes of public rejoicing. However, in January 1999 rebel groups, mainly from the AFRC/former Sierra

Leonean army, again attacked and occupied most of Freetown. During this invasion and occupation, over 5,000 people were killed and most of the eastern suburbs destroyed. ECOMOG forces eventually forced the rebels out of the capital and a cease-fire was agreed to in May 1999. This led to the Lomé Peace Accord signed on 7 July 1999. Ten months of relative stability ensued. In May 2000, United Nations peacekeeping forces came under attack in the east of the country from RUF rebels who also were closing in on the capital. The RUF leader Foday Sankoh was captured, however, and on 10 November 2000, the government of Sierra Leone and the RUF signed a cease-fire agreement.

In January 2002 the war was declared over and the United Nations confirmed that the disarmament of 45,000 fighters was complete. More than 17,000 foreign troops were engaged in this process and it represents the biggest United Nations peacekeeping success in Africa for many years.

SOUTH AFRICA

Population (2001): 43.8 million of whom 17.6 million are under 18 (UNICEF)

Secondary school enrollment 2000–2001: 87 percent (gross) or 57 percent (net) (UNESCO)

Percentage of population aged 15–24 who are illiterate: 8.7 percent (UNESCO)

Life expectancy: 45 years (men), 51 years (women) (UN)

Average annual income (2001): US$2,820 (World Bank)

Capital: Pretoria

Until 1994, South Africa was ruled by a white minority. The all-white National Party, in power since 1948, passed successive legislation codifying and enforcing a strict policy of white domination and racial separation known as apartheid.

In September 1984, serious riots broke out that were violently repressed by security forces and in July 1985 a state of emergency was declared. In June 1986, a new state of emergency was declared that restricted the media. African National Congress (ANC) guerrilla campaigns escalated and young blacks, also known as "Comrades," began to kill other blacks suspected of cooperating with the whites or refusing to join their campaign. In January 1989, Prime Minister Botha resigned after suffering a stroke and was replaced by F. W. de Klerk.

The sporadic popular uprisings in black and colored townships since 1976 had helped to convince some National Party members of the need for change. Prime Minister de Klerk began to establish social reforms. In February 1990, the ANC, Pan-African Congress (PAC), and South African Communist Party (SACP) were again legalized. Nelson Mandela was released from prison after 27 years.

In June 1990, violence erupted between the ANC and Inkatha Freedom Party (IFP) led by Zulu chief Mangosuthu Buthelezi. In August 1990, the government met with the ANC, who demanded an interim government as well as a new constitution based on a single vote for every citizen. In January 1991, the ANC and IFP signed a peace agreement, although clashes between the groups continued. In February 1991, President de Klerk announced major reforms for the new South Africa; 20,000 demonstrators in Cape Town demanded the abolition of apartheid laws. In June 1991, the Group Areas Act, Land Acts, and the Population Registration Act, the last of the so-called "pillars of apartheid," were abolished. A long series of negotiations ensued, resulting in a new constitution passed into law in December 1993. The country's first nonracial elections were held in April 1994, and Nelson Mandela became president in May 1994.

Sri Lanka

Population (2001): 19 million of whom 6 million are under 18 (UNICEF)

Secondary school enrollment 2000–2001: 72 percent (gross, no net figures available) (UNESCO)

Percentage of population aged 15–24 who are illiterate: 3.2 percent (UNESCO)

Life expectancy: 70 years (men), 76 years (women) (UN)

Average annual income (2001): US$880 (World Bank)

Capital: Colombo

Since gaining independence from the United Kingdom in 1948, historical divisions continue to have an impact on Sri Lankan society and politics. The island has a mainly Hindu/Tamil minority whom, under the British administration, the majority Buddhist/Sinhalese community resented for what they saw as favoritism. The growth of a more assertive Sinhala nationalism after independence fanned the flames of these ethnic divisions leading, in the early 1980s, to a protracted civil war.

In the 1977 elections, the Tamil United Liberation Front (TULF) won all the seats in Tamil areas on a platform of separatism. Other groups, particularly the Liberation Tigers of Tamil Eelam (LTTE), sought an independent state by armed struggle. In 1983, the killing of 13 Sinhalese soldiers by the LTTE led to rioting and reprisal against Tamils living in the south. In mid-1987, the Indo-Sri Lankan Peace Accord provided for an Indian Peacekeeping Force (IPKF) and led to a controversial amendment of the constitution introducing the provincial council system as an attempt to devolve power. There was heavy fighting and reports of human rights violations on both sides. Within weeks, the LTTE declared its intent to continue its armed struggle for an independent Tamil Eelam and refused to disarm. From April 1989 to June 1990, the government engaged in direct communications with the LTTE leadership. India withdrew the last of its forces from Sri Lanka in May 1990 and fighting between the LTTE and the government resumed. The LTTE extended their area of control until they held both the Jaffna peninsula and large areas of the north and east. The security forces succeeded in winning back most of the east, but the north remained outside their control.

In July 1995, the Sri Lankan army launched a military operation, culminating in the fall of Jaffna in December 1995 to government forces. At the end of January 1996 a bombing campaign, allegedly the work of the LTTE, began in Colombo. During 1996, the Sri Lankan army managed to secure enough of the Jaffna Peninsula to make it possible for the Tamil civilian population to return to Jaffna town. However the LTTE reasserted themselves in the eastern province and infiltrated back into the Jaffna Peninsula. Terrorist attacks continued in the capital of Colombo. In March 1999, the Sri Lankan army launched two major offensives in the Vanni and captured over 800 square kilometers of territory from the LTTE. Fighting in the north intensified in late 1999 and the Vanni fell to the LTTE. In April 2000, the LTTE carried out a major assault leading to the withdrawal of Sri Lankan troops from a major base, Elephant Pass. With control of Elephant Pass, the LTTE continued further attacks into the Jaffna Peninsula.

The LTTE announced a cease-fire from 24 December 2000, which they extended until 24 April 2001, and fighting was limited during this time. However, July 2001 saw a major attack within the immediate vicinity of the Colombo International Airport, which dramatically affected the Sri Lankan economy. Sporadic fighting then continued until 24 December 2001 when the LTTE announced a new cease-fire, which the newly elected United National Front (UNF) government reciprocated. In February 2002, the government and the LTTE signed a permanent cease-fire agreement paving the way for talks to end the conflict. The peace initiative is sponsored by Norway.

Note

1. Crown copyright material is reproduced with the permission of the Controller of HMSO.

Bibliography

Aarsman, Irma. 1993. *The Shona People in Southern Zimbabwe,* unpublished thesis (Utrecht, Netherlands: University of Utrecht).

Achio, Françoise, and Irma Specht. 2003. "Youth in Conflict." In Eugenia Date-Bah (ed.), *Jobs After War* (Geneva: ILO), pp. 153–166.

African Charter on the Rights and Welfare of the Child. OAU Doc. CAB/LEG/24.9/49 1990.

Amnesty International. 2000. *United Kingdom: U-18s: Report on the Recruitment and Deployment of Child Soldiers,* November, AI index EUR 45/057/2000.

———. 2003. *Democratic Republic of Congo: Children at War,* AI index AFR 62/034/2003.

Beirens, Hanne. 2002. *Reflections on the Methodology of the South Africa Pilot Study: ILO Voices of Young Soldiers Research Project* (Warwick, England: University of Warwick).

Bennett, Allison. 2002. *The Reintegration of Child Ex-Combatants in Sierra Leone with Particular Focus on the Needs of Females,* unpublished dissertation (London: University of East London).

Bernstein, Susan R. 1991. *Managing Contracted Services in the Nonprofit Agency: Administrative, Ethical and Political Issues* (Philadelphia, PA: Temple University Press).

Bogdan, Robert C., and Sari Knopp Bilken. 1982. *Qualitative Research for Education: An Introduction to Theory and Methods* (Boston, MA: Allyn & Bacon).

Brett, Rachel, and Margaret McCallin. 1998. *Children: The Invisible Soldiers,* 2nd edition (Stockholm: Rädda Barnen).

Bush, Kenneth, and Diana Saltarelli. 2000. *The Two Faces of Education in Ethnic Conflict. Towards a Peacebuilding Education for Children,* August (Florence: UNICEF Innocenti Research Centre).

Cagoco-Guiam, Rufa. 2002. *Philippines—Child Soldiers in Central and Western Mindanao: A Rapid Assessment.* In the IPEC series *Investigating the Worst Forms of Child Labour* (Geneva: ILO).

Cairns, Ed. 1996. *Children and Political Violence* (London: Blackwell).

179

Cairns, Ed, and Tara Cairns. 1995. "Children and Conflict: A Psychological Perspective." In Seamus Dunn (ed.), *Facets of the Conflict in Northern Ireland* (Houndmills: Macmillan), pp. 97–113.

Camacho, Agnes Zenaida V., Faye A. G. Balanon, and Arlyn G. Verba. 2001. *Children Involved in the Armed Conflict in the Philippines.* Case studies of child soldiers in the New Peoples' Army, a UNICEF Project (Manila: University of the Philippines, Program on Psychosocial Trauma and Human Rights, Centre for Integrative and Development Studies).

Chung, Fay. 1999. "Education: A Key to Power and a Tool for Change: A Practitioner's Perspective," *Current Issues in Comparative Education* 2, no. 1: 1–6.

Coalition to Stop the Use of Child Soldiers. 2001. "Child Soldiers Global Report": www.child-soldiers.org/.

———. 2002. "Child Soldiers 1379 Report": www.child-soldiers.org/.

Crill, M. 2000. *The Demobilisation and Reintegration of Former Child Soldiers in the Democratic Republic of Congo.* A Consultancy Report for Save the Children UK (London: Save the Children).

David, Kelly. 1998. *The Disarmament, Demobilization and Reintegration of Child Soldiers in Liberia, 1994–1997: The Processes and Lessons Learned* (UNICEF-Liberia and the U.S. National Committee for UNICEF).

de Silva, D.G.H., and C. J. Hobbs. 2001. "Conscription of Children in Armed Conflict," *British Medical Journal* 322: 1372.

Dumas, Laetitia, and Michaëlle de Cock. 2003. *Wounded Childhood: The Use of Child Soldiers in Armed Conflict in Central Africa* (Geneva: ILO).

Ellis, Stephen. 2001. *The Masks of Anarchy: The Destruction of Liberia and the Religious Dimension of an African Civil War* (New York: New York University Press).

English, Richard. 2003. *Armed Struggle: A History of the IRA* (London: Macmillan).

Erikson, Erik H. 1972. *Adolescence et crise: la quête de l'identité* (Paris: Flammarion).

Goldberg, Jeffrey. 2000. "Inside Jihad U.: The Education of a Holy Warrior," *New York Times Magazine,* 25 June, section 6, pp. 32–37.

Goodwin-Gill, Guy, and Ilene Cohn. 1994. *Child Soldiers* (Oxford: Oxford University Press).

Guba, Egon G., and Yvonna S. Lincoln. 1994. "Competing Paradigms in Qualitative Research." In Norman Denzin and Yvonna Lincoln (eds.), *Handbook of Qualitative Research* (Newbury Park, CA: Sage), pp. 105–117.

Haar, Gerrie ter. 1997. *Report on Social Cultural Factors in Liberia,* unpublished ILO mission report (Geneva: ILO).

Herman, Judith. 1997. *Trauma and Recovery* (New York: Basic Books).

Honwana, Alcinda. 1999. "Negocier les identités d'après-guerre: le cas des enfants soldats au Mozambique et en Angola," *Bulletin du CODESRIA* 1 and 2: 4–14.

Human Rights Watch. 2002. *My Gun Was As Tall As Me: Child Soldiers in Burma,* October (New York).

———. 2003. *You'll Learn Not to Cry: Child Combatants in Colombia,* September (New York).

International Criminal Court. 1998. Rome Statute of the International Criminal Court, Rome, 17 July.

International Labour Organization. 1995a. *Reintegrating Demobilized Combat-ants: Experiences from Four African Countries.* Report presented at the Expert Meeting on the Design of Guidelines for Training and Employment of Ex-Combatants (Africa Region), Harare, Zimbabwe, 11–14 July.

———. 1995b. *Reintegrating Demobilized Combatants: The Role of Small Enterprise Development* (Geneva).

———. 1995c. *The Reintegration of Young Ex-Combatants into Civilian Life.* Report presented at the Expert Meeting on the Design of Guidelines for Training and Employment of Ex-Combatants (Africa Region), Harare, Zimbabwe, 11–14 July.

———. 1997. *Guidelines for Employment and Skills Training in Conflict-Affected Countries* (Geneva).

———. 2002. *Key Indicators of the Labour Market 2001* (Geneva).

———. *Report of the Committee of Experts on the Applications of Conventions and Recommendations,* Report III (Part 1A), International Labour Conference, Individual Observations concerning Convention No. 29, Forced Labour, 1930: Brazil (88th Session, 2000); Iraq (89th Session, 2001); Sudan (85th Session, 1997); Burundi (90th Session, 2002); Democratic Republic of Congo (90th Session, 2002); Uganda (90th Session, 2002).

Isaksson, Eva (ed.). 1988. *Women and the Military System* (New York: Harvester Wheatsheaf).

Jancar, Barbara. 1988. "Women Soldiers in Yugoslavia's National Liberation Struggle, 1941–1945." In Eva Isaksson (ed.), *Women and the Military System* (New York: Harvester Wheatsheaf), pp. 47–67.

Janesick, Valerie J. 1994. "The Dance of Qualitative Research Design: Metaphor, Methodolatry and Meaning." In Norman Denzin and Yvonna Lincoln (eds.), *Handbook of Qualitative Research,* 1st edition (Newbury Park, CA: Sage), pp. 209–219.

Keairns, Yvonne E. 2002. *The Voices of Girl Child Soldiers: Summary.* October (New York and Geneva: Quaker United Nations Office).

———. 2003a. *The Voices of Girl Child Soldiers: Colombia.* January (New York and Geneva: Quaker United Nations Office).

———. 2003b. *The Voices of Girl Child Soldiers: Philippines.* January (New York and Geneva: Quaker United Nations Office).

———. 2003c. *The Voices of Girl Child Soldiers: Sri Lanka.* January. (New York and Geneva: Quaker United Nations Office).

Lindsay, Charlotte. 2001. *Women Facing War: ICRC Study on the Impact of Armed Conflict on Women* (Geneva: ICRC).

Lobner, Sabine. 1997. *Life Skills for the World of Work: Experiences of South Africa* (Geneva: ILO).

Machel, Graça. 1996. *Impact of Armed Conflict on Children.* Report of the expert of the Secretary-General submitted pursuant to General Assembly Resolution 48/157. UN Document A/51/306 and Add.1. (New York: United Nations).

———. 2001. *The Impact of War on Children* (London: Hurst & Company).

———. 2003. *The Impact of War on Children: A Review of Progress Since the 1996 United Nations Report on the Impact of Armed Conflict on Children.* March (New York: United Nations).

McCallin, Margaret. 1998. "Community Involvement in the Social Reintegration of Child Soldiers." In P. J. Bracken and C. Petty (eds.), *Rethinking the Trauma of War* (New York: Free Association Books Ltd.), pp. 60–75.

McConnan, Isobel, and Sarah Uppard. 2001. *Children—Not Soldiers* (London: Save the Children).

McKay, Susan, and Dyan Mazurana. 2000. "Girls in Militaries, Paramilitaries, and Armed Opposition Groups," paper prepared for the War Affected Children Conference, Winnipeg, 10–17 September.

McManners, Hugh. 1994. *The Scars of War* (London: HarperCollins).

Mintzberg, Henry. 1983. "An Emerging Strategy of 'Direct Research.'" In John Van Maanen (ed.), *Qualitative Research* (Newbury Park, CA: Sage), pp. 117–134.

Mjøset, Lars, and Stephen van Holde. 2002. "Killing for the State, Dying for the Nation: An Introductory Essay on the Life Cycle of Conscription into Europe's Armed Forces." In L. Mjøset and S. van Holde (eds.), *The Comparative Study of Conscription in the Armed Forces,* Comparative Social Research Series, vol. 20 (Greenwich, CT: JAI), pp. 3–94.

Nordstrom, Carolyn. 1997. *Girls and War Zones: Troubling Questions* (Uppsala, Sweden: Life and Peace Institute).

Otunnu, Olara. 1999. *Protection of Children Affected by Armed Conflict: Note by the Secretary-General.* Report prepared by Olara A. Otunnu, Special Representative of the Secretary-General for Children and Armed Conflict. UN Document A/54/430 (New York: United Nations).

Páez, Erika. 2001. *Girls in the Colombian Armed Groups: A Diagnosis* (Osnabruck, Germany: Terre des Hommes).

Patton, Michael. 1990. *Qualitative Evaluation and Research Methods,* 2nd edition (Newbury Park, CA: Sage).

Peters, Krijn, and Paul Richards. 1998a. "Fighting with Open Eyes: Youth Combatants Talking About War in Sierra Leone." In P. J. Bracken and C. Petty (eds.), *Rethinking the Trauma of War* (New York: Free Association Books Ltd.), pp. 76–111.

———. 1998b. "Why We Fight: Voices of Youth Combatants in Sierra Leone," *Africa* 68, no. 2: 183–210.

Poulton, Robin-Edward, and Ibrahim Youssouf. 1998. *A Peace of Timbuktu: Democratic Governance, Development and African Peacemaking* (Geneva: United Nations Institute for Disarmament Research).

Ragin, Charles. 1994. *Constructing Social Research: The Unity and Diversity of Method* (Thousand Oaks, CA: Pine Forge).

Richards, Paul. 1996. *Fighting for the Rain Forest: War, Youth and Resources in Sierra Leone* (Oxford: The International African Institute in association with James Currey).

———. 2002. "Militia Conscription in Sierra Leone: Recruitment of Young Fighters in an African War." In L. Mjøset and S. van Holde (eds.), *The Comparative Study of Conscription in the Armed Forces,* Comparative Social Research Series, vol. 20 (Greenwich, CT: JAI), pp. 255–276.

Ritter, Gretchen. 2002. "Of War and Virtue: Gender, American Citizenship and Veterans' Benefits After World War II." In L. Mjøset and S. van Holde (eds.), *The Comparative Study of Conscription in the Armed Forces,* Comparative Social Research Series, vol. 20 (Greenwich, CT: JAI), pp. 201–226.

Schatzman, Leonard, and Anselm Strauss. 1973. *Field Research: Strategies for a Natural Sociology* (Englewood Cliffs, NJ: Prentice Hall).

Seidman, Irving. 1998. *Interviewing as Qualitative Research: A Guide for Researchers in Education and Social Sciences.* 2nd edition (New York: Teachers College Press).

Shepler, Susan. 2002. "Les filles-soldats: Trajectories d'après-guerre en Sierra Leone," *Politique Africaine* 88: 49–62.

———. Forthcoming. "Globalizing Child Soldiers in Sierra Leone." In S. Maira and E. Soep (eds.), *Youthscapes: Popular Cultures, National Ideologies, Global Markets.*

Sierra Leone National Committee for Disarmament, Demobilization and Reintegration (NCDDR). 2002. *Reintegration of Ex-Combatants* (Freetown, Sierra Leone: NCDDR).

Sommers, Marc. 2002. *Children, Education and War: Reaching Education for All (EFA) Objectives in Countries Affected by Conflict.* Working Paper No. 1, World Bank Conflict Prevention and Reconstruction Unit (Washington, DC: World Bank).

Specht, Irma, and Carlien Empel. 1998. *Enlargement—A Challenge for Social and Economic Reintegration: Targeting Ex-Combatants or All War-Affected People? The Liberian Experience.* IFP/CRISIS Report (Geneva: ILO).

Spencer, Denise. 1997. *Demobilization and Reintegration in Central America,* Paper 8 (Bonn: Bonn International Center for Conversion).

Srivastava, Ramesh. 1994. *Reintegrating Demobilized Combatants: A Report Exploring Options and Strategies for Training-Related Interventions* (Geneva: ILO).

Susman, Tina. 1999. "Dual Captivity: Rebel Groups Force Girls into Soldiering and Sex," *NY Newsday,* 11 October, p. A5.

Susman, Tina, and Geoffrey Mohan. 1999. "A Generation Lost to War," *NY Newsday,* 23 October, p. A6.

Tagg, Stephen, K. 1985. "Life Story Interviews and Their Interpretations." In M. Brenner, J. Brown, and D. Canter (eds.), *The Research Interview: Uses and Approaches* (London: Academic), pp. 163–199.

Terkel, Studs. 1972. *Working* (New York: New).

Thompson, Carol B. 1999. "Beyond Civil Society: Child Soldiers as Citizens in Mozambique," *Review of African Political Economy* 26, no. 80: 191–206.

United Nations. 1977a. Protocol Additional to the Geneva Conventions of 12 August 1949, and relating to the Protection of Victims of International Armed Conflicts (Protocol I), 8 June 1977.

———. 1977b. Protocol Additional to the Geneva Conventions of 12 August 1949, and relating to the Protection of Victims of Non-International Armed Conflicts (Protocol II), 8 June 1977.

———. 1989. Convention on the Rights of the Child. 1989. Annex to United Nations General Assembly Resolution A/RES/44/25, 12 December.

———. 2000. Optional Protocol to the Convention on the Rights of the Child on the Involvement of Children in Armed Conflict. 25 May 2000 (General Assembly Resolution A/Res/54/263).

———. 2003. *World Youth Report.* Report of the Secretary-General. UN Document E/CN.5/2003/4.

United Nations Children's Fund (UNICEF). 2000. *The Demobilization and Reintegration of Child Soldiers: Lessons Learned from Angola and El Salvador* (New York: UNICEF).

———. 2002. *Adult Wars, Child Soldiers: Voices of Children Involved in Armed Conflict in East Asia and Pacific Region* (Bangkok: UNICEF East Asia and Pacific Regional Office).

United Nations Department of Peacekeeping Operations, Lessons Learned Unit. 1996. *Multidisciplinary Peacekeeping: Lessons from Recent Experience* (New York: United Nations).

———. 2000. *Disarmament, Demobilization and Reintegration of Ex-Combatants in a Peacekeeping Environment: Principles and Guidelines* (New York: United Nations).

United Nations Organization for the Coordination of Humanitarian Affairs (UNOCHA). 2002. *Consolidated Inter-Agency Appeal for Sierra Leone 2002* (Geneva: UNOCHA).

United Nations Security Council, Resolution S/RES/1261 on the Use of Children as Soldiers. 1999.

Van Maanen, John. 1983. "The Fact of Fiction in Organizational Ethnography." In John Van Maanen (ed.), *Qualitative Research* (Beverley Hills, CA: Sage), pp. 37–55.

Veale, Angela. 2003. *From Child Soldier to Ex-Fighter: Female Fighters, Demobilisation and Reintegration in Ethiopia,* ISS Monograph No. 85 (Pretoria: Institute of Security Studies).

Verhey, Beth. 2003. *Going Home: Demobilising and Reintegrating Child Soldiers in the Democratic Republic of the Congo* (London: Save the Children UK).

Wax, Rosalie. 1971. "The Ambiguities of Fieldwork." In Robert Emerson (ed.), *Contemporary Field Research: A Collection of Readings* (Prospect Heights, IL: Waveland), reissued 1988, pp. 191–202.

Werbner, Richard, and Terence Ranger (eds.). 1996. *Post-Colonial Identities in Africa* (London and New Jersey: Zed Books Ltd.).

Werner, Emmy E. 1998. *Reluctant Witnesses: Children's Voices from the Civil War* (Boulder, CO: Westview).

Wessells, Michael. 2002. "Recruitment of Children as Soldiers in Sub-Saharan Africa: An Ecological Analysis." In L. Mjøset and S. van Holde (eds.), *The Comparative Study of Conscription in the Armed Forces,* Comparative Social Research Series, vol. 20 (Greenwich, CT: JAI), pp. 237–254.

Women's Commission for Refugee Women and Children. 2000. *Untapped Potential: Adolescents Affected by Armed Conflict: A Review of Programs and Policies.* January (New York).

———. 2002. *Precious Resources: Adolescents in the Reconstruction of Sierra Leone.* Participatory research study with adolescents and youth in Sierra Leone, April–July 2002 (New York).

World Bank. 1993. *Demobilization and Reintegration of Military Personnel in Africa: The Evidence from Seven Country Case Studies.* Discussion paper, Africa Regional Series, Report No. IDP-130 (Washington, DC: World Bank).

World Bank/Carter Center. 1997. *From Civil War to Civil Society. The Transition from War to Peace in Guatemala and Liberia.* Report from a workshop series on the transition from war to peace, Atlanta, Georgia, 19–21 February.

Zack-Williams, A. B. 2001. "Child Soldiers in the Civil War in Sierra Leone."
In *Review of African Political Economy* 28, no. 87: 73–82.

Internet Sources

www.mod.uk/aboutus/factfiles/cadets.htm [consulted 05 May 2003]
www.rfca.org.uk/tav_rmc.htm [consulted 05 May 2003]
www.mod.uk/aboutus/factfiles/community.htm [consulted 05 May 2003]
www.state.gov Background Notes [consulted 06 July 2003]
www.bbc.co.uk [consulted 06 July 2003]
www.fco.gov.uk Country Profiles [consulted 06 July 2003]
www.odci.gov/cia The World Fact Book [consulted 06 July 2003]
www.wikipedia.org [consulted 06 July 2003]
www.atlapedia.com [consulted 06 July 2003]
www.Cain.ulst.ac.uk [consulted 06 July 2003]
www.reliefweb.int [consulted 06 July 2003]

Index

Aarsman, Irma, 101
Abuse, domestic exploitation and, 88–91, 95
Adolescence, specific features of, 2–3, 29–32
Afghanistan: adolescence, specific features of, 30; conflict profile, 163–164; critical moment of making decision/responding to crisis, 65–66; culture/tradition of violence/warfare, 32, 33; education/training/employment, 19, 45; family/social support networks, 25, 50; guns, availability/familiarity with, 13; military/parties to the conflict influencing youth involvement, 11, 57–58; politics and ideology, 28, 29; reflective thoughts of young soldier, 121; research and methodological issues, 141; risk factors common to young soldiers linked, 77–79; vignette, personal, 6–7; volunteering concept, 106
African Charter on the Rights and Welfare of the Child, 113, 117
African National Congress (ANC), 175. *See also* South Africa
Alliance of Democratic Forces for the Liberation of Congo-Zaire (AFDL), 169. *See also* Democratic Republic of Congo
Angola, cleansing child soldiers in, 101
Apartheid, 175–176. *See also* South Africa
Armed Forces Revolutionary Council (AFRC), 173–174. *See also* Sierra Leone

Assumptions about young soldiers, challenging, 1–2

Bantu Education Act, 17
Betancur, Belisario, 165
Bio, Julius M., 173
Botha, P. W., 175
Buthelezi, Mangosuthu, 175

Cadet programs,19, 54, 61–62
Cleansing child soldiers, demobilization/ reintegration and, 101
Colombia: adolescence, specific features of, 30–32; conflict profile, 165–166; critical moment of making decision/responding to crisis, 70; culture/tradition of violence/warfare, 33; domestic exploitation/abuse, 88–90; economic motivations, 43; education/ training/employment, 44, 45–46, 96; family/social support networks, 24, 48–50; girls and boys, 86, 93, 96–98; guns, availability/familiarity with, 13; military/parties to the conflict influencing youth involvement, 56; peer influence, 51–52; politics and ideology, 60–61; poverty, 14; recruitment of young soldiers, 72; research and methodological issues, 141; role-models, soldiers/militants as, 92–93; self-protection, feeling the need for, 40; violent behavior legitimized by living in context of armed violence, 12
Committee of Experts on the Application of Conventions and Recommendations,

186

ILO's, 112, 113
Committee on the Rights of the Child, 115
Conflict profiles: Afghanistan, 163–164; Colombia, 165–166; Congo-Brazzaville, 167–168; Democratic Republic of Congo, 169–170; Ireland, Northern, 171–172; Sierra Leone, 173–174; South Africa, 175–176; Sri Lanka, 177–178
Congo. *See* Congo-Brazzaville; Democratic Republic of Congo (DRC)
Congo-Brazzaville: adolescence, specific features of, 30, 31; conflict profile, 167–168; critical moment of making decision/responding to crisis, 67, 69; demobilization and reintegration, 133; economic motivations, 43, 44; education/training/employment, 21–22, 46; media and culture/tradition of violence/warfare, 35, 92; military/parties to the conflict influencing youth involvement, 12, 57, 58; parental consent, 116; peer influence, 26, 52; politics and ideology, 29; poverty, 15; reflective thoughts of a young soldier, 136; research and methodological issues, 140, 141; self-protection, feeling the need for, 13, 40, 95
Congress of South African Students (COSAS), 21
Country profiles. *See* Conflict profiles; *individual countries*
Critical moment of making decision/responding to crisis: conclusions/summary, 73–74, 135–136; family events, 68–71; outbreak of violence, 65–67; peer group influence, 71; recruitment, 71–73; school, 67–68; vignette, personal: Sri Lanka, 75
Culture/tradition of violence/warfare, 31–36, 81, 86–87
Cut and paste style research method, 148

Data. *See* Research *listings*
de Klerk, F. W., 175
Demobilization and reintegration, 5, 98–102, 129–135
Democratic Republic of Congo (DRC): conflict profile, 169–170; demobilization and reintegration, 99, 131, 132, 134, 135; domestic exploitation/abuse, 88; economic motivations, 43; education/training/

employment, 20; family/social support networks, 24, 25, 50–51; girls and boys, 85, 86, 98, 99; irrevocable nature of the decision, not realizing, 110; media and culture/tradition of violence/warfare, 36; options, joining armed groups because of lack of other, 41; parental consent, 116; peer influence, 52; politics and ideology, 27, 28, 60; poverty, 14; recruitment of young soldiers, 56, 72; research and methodological issues, 140, 141; roles/expectations, societal, 91; self-protection, feeling the need for, 13, 40, 95; volunteering concept, 108, 109
Domestic exploitation/abuse, 88–91, 95

East Timor: demobilization and reintegration, 133; girls and boys, 86, 87, 95, 98
Economic Community of West African States Monitoring Group (ECOMOG), 173
Economic motivations, 41–44. *See also* Poverty as a factor leading to young soldiers
Education/training/employment: battleground for hearts/minds of students, school as, 19–21; critical moment of making decision/responding to crisis, 67–68; demobilization and reintegration, 129–134; girls and boys, 82, 96–97, 101; labor demand fluctuations, 21–23; overview, 15–16, 23; quality of education system, 17–18; recruitment easier with uneducated youngsters, 44–47; risk factors common to young soldiers linked, 79, 80–81; summary identifying it as key factor in research, 125–127; volunteering concept, 107–108
El Salvador and girls and boys, 97, 99
Employment. *See* Education/training/employment
Environmental factors leading to involvement of young soldiers: adolescence, specific features of, 29–32; conclusions/summary, 36; culture/tradition of violence/warfare, 32–36; education and employment, 15–23; family/social support networks, 23–26; overview, 9; politics and ideology, 27–29; poverty, 14–15; three levels of, 3–4; war, 9–14. *See also* Critical

moment of making decision/
responding to crisis; Risk factors
common to young soldiers linked;
Individual young persons, impacts on
Erikson, Erik, 29
Escape from home, war offering an,
13–14, 32, 48–49, 106
Ethics, research, 159–162
Ethnicity/race, 13, 87

Factors making young people vulnerable
to military participation: education/
training/employment, 125–127; family,
124–125; overview, 121–123; peer
influence, 128; poverty, 127–128; war,
124–125. *See also* Critical moment of
making decision/responding to crisis;
Environmental factors leading to
involvement of young soldiers; Risk
factors common to young soldiers
linked; Individual young persons,
impacts on
Family/social support networks:
adolescence, specific features of, 31;
critical moment of making decision/
responding to crisis, 68–71; demobilization and reintegration, 134–135;
domestic exploitation/abuse, 88–89;
escape from home, war offering an,
48–49; following/imitating other family
members, 50–51; girls and boys, 93,
95; overview, 23–25; parental consent,
116; preventing members from joining
conflict, 51; risk factors common to
young soldiers linked, 80; roles/
expectations, societal, 92; summary
identifying it as key factor in research,
124–125; volunteering concept, 107;
war disrupting, 13. *See also* Peer group
influence
Forced Labour Convention No. 29
(1930), 112. *See also* Recruitment of
young soldiers; Volunteering, the
concept of

Gender issues/distinctions. *See* Girls and
boys
Girls and boys: conclusions/summary,
100–102; cultural extremes involving
girls in conflicts, 86–87;
demobilization and reintegration,
98–100; domestic exploitation/abuse,
88–91; education/training/employment,
82, 96–97; escape from home, war

offering an, 14; overview, 85–86;
protection for self and family, 93,
95–96; reaction to involvement, 97–98;
religion and ethnicity, 87; roles/
expectations, societal, 91–93; self-
protection, feeling the need for, 13
Guevara, Che, 92
Guns, war leading to availability/
familiarity with, 13, 33

Historical context for young soldiers,
81–82
HIV/AIDS, 101
Honwana, Alcinda, 101
Hutu people, 169

Identity, adolescent searching for an, 30,
53–54
Individual young persons, impacts on:
conclusions/summary, 62–63; economic
motivations, 41–44; education, 44–47;
family/social support networks, 48–54;
military/parties to the conflict, 54–58;
politics and ideology, 58–62; war and
insecurity, 39–41. *See also* Critical
moment of making decision/responding
to crisis; Risk factors common to
young soldiers linked
Indo-Sri Lankan Peace Accord (1987),
177
InFocus Programme on Crisis Response
and Reconstruction (IFP/CRISIS), 137
Informants approach as survey
methodology, 142–143
Informed consent for interviewees,
161–162
Inkatha Freedom Party (IFP), 175
International Labour Organization (ILO):
Convention No. 29, 112; Convention
No. 182, 138; girls and boys, 87;
Infocus Programme on Crisis Response
and Reconstruction, 137; legal issues
around concept of volunteering, 112,
114, 115; research and methodological
issues, 138; volunteering of child
soldiers, 1
Interviewing. *See* Researchers,
instructions provided to
Invulnerability, adolescents having
feelings of, 30
Ireland, Northern: adolescence, specific
features of, 31, 32; conflict profile,
171–172; critical moment of making
decision/responding to crisis, 65;

economic motivations, 42; education/
training/employment, 16, 17, 22, 45;
girls and boys, 86; leave, recruits not
allowed to, 110; military/parties to the
conflict influencing youth involvement,
11, 12, 56, 58, 93; options, joining
armed groups because of lack of other,
41; peer influence, 26, 53; politics and
ideology, 28; recruitment of young
soldiers, 72; research and
methodological issues, 141; role-
models, soldiers/militants as, 93; self-
protection, feeling the need for, 40–41;
violent behavior legitimized by living
in context of armed violence, 12
Irish Republican Army (IRA), 171–172.
See also Ireland, Northern

Kabila, Joseph, 170
Kabila, Laurent, 169, 170
Khan, Esmail, 6
Kolelas, Bernard, 167
Koroma, Johnny P., 173

Leave, recruits not allowed to, 110, 111,
128–129
Legal issues around concept of
volunteering, 112–117
Liberation Tigers of Tamil Eelam (LTTE),
177–178
Linguistic differences and the interview
process, 154–155
Lomé Peace Accord (1999), 174

Maada Bio, Julius, 173
Machel, Graça, 3
Mandela, Nelson, 175, 176
Manhood, beliefs about, 31–32
Masks of Anarchy, The (Ellis), 1
Media and culture/tradition of violence/
warfare, 33, 35–36, 92
Medical services expected to be provided
by girls, 98
Military/parties to the conflict influencing
youth involvement, 10–12, 54–58,
92–93
Mjøset, Lars, 81
Momoh, Joseph, 173
Mozambique, cleansing child soldiers in,
101

Najibollah, Dr., 6
National Liberation Army (ELN),
165–166. *See also* Colombia

Netherlands, Ministry of Foreign Affairs
of the Kingdom of the, 137
Norway and Sri Lanka, 178

Omar, Mullah, 163
Optional Protocol to the Convention on
the Rights of the Child on Involvement
of Children in Armed Conflicts (2000),
114–115
Options, joining armed groups because of
lack of other, 41, 106, 108

Páez, Erika, 82, 89
Pakistan: critical moment of making
decision/responding to crisis, 68,
70–71; economic motivations, 43;
education/training/employment, 19, 23,
46, 47; family/social support networks,
24, 50; girls and boys, 86; media and
culture/tradition of violence/warfare,
35; peer group influence, 51–53;
politics and ideology, 28, 59–61;
reflective thoughts of young soldier,
121; research and methodological
issues, 141; roles/expectations, societal,
92; volunteering concept, 105, 106, 109
Parental consent, 114, 115, 116
Pastrana Arango, Andres, 166
Peer group influence: critical moment of
making decision/responding to crisis,
71; identity development, 53–54;
overview, 25–26, 51–53; risk factors
common to young soldiers linked, 81;
summary identifying it as key factor in
research, 128
Philippines: family/social support
networks, 125; girls and boys, 86, 87,
89–91, 98; leave, recruits not allowed
to, 110; volunteering concept, 107
Politics and ideology, 27–29, 58–62
Poverty as a factor leading to young
soldiers: complex factor, 3–4, 15; long-
standing condition, 14; risk factors
common to young soldiers linked, 79;
starvation, 41–42; summary identifying
it as key factor in research, 127–128;
volunteering concept, 107; war creating
poverty, 14
Propaganda, adolescents influenced by,
30
Protocol to Prevent, Suppress and Punish
Trafficking in Persons, Especially
Women and Children, 115, 117

Quaker United Nations Office, 137, 144

Race/ethnicity, 13, 87
Reciprocity and the interview process, 156
Recruitment of young soldiers: cadet programs, 54, 61–62; critical moment of making decision/responding to crisis, 71–73; education (lack of) leading to easier, 44–47; forced and voluntary recruitment, distinction between, 83; Optional Protocol to the Convention on the Rights of the Child on Involvement of Children in Armed Conflicts (2000), 115; poverty, 41–42; self-protection, 40–41, 56; video tapes, 54–55; Worst Forms of Child Labour Convention No. 182 (1999), 113, 114; young people initiating the contact, 55, 56. *See also* Volunteering, the concept of
Reintegration, demobilization and, 5, 98–102, 129–135
Religion, 13, 19, 28, 87
Republic of Congo. *See* Congo-Brazzaville
Research and methodological issues: analysis/interpretation of data, 147–149; case studies, 139–142; data, the primary, 144–146; data collection, 143–144; informants, selection of, 37(note 3), 142–143; project proposal, 137–139
Researchers, instructions provided to: data collection, guide for, 149–150; ethics, 159–162; interviews, principles for the, 151–156; outputs and reporting, 157–158; participants and security, selection of, 150–151; responsibilities, actions and, 158–160; topics list for the open interviews, 156–157
Revolutionary Armed Forces of Colombia (FARC), 165–166. *See also* Colombia
Revolutionary United Front (RUF), 173–174. *See also* Sierra Leone
Risk factors common to young soldiers, linking: conclusions/summary, 82–83; education/training/employment, 80–81; family, 80; forced and voluntary recruitment, distinction between, 83; historical context, 81–82; Mjøset (Lars) and van Holde (Stephen), 81; overview, 79–80; vary in different situations, 82; vignette, personal: Afghanistan, 77–79; war, 80

Ritter, Gretchen, 101
Role models, soldiers/militants as, 92–93, 101
Roles/expectations, societal, 91–93
Rwanda, 169–170. *See also* Democratic Republic of Congo

Sassou-Nguesso, Denis, 167
School. *See* Education/training/employment
Self-protection, feeling the need for, 13, 40–41, 56, 93, 95–96
Sexual abuse, 90, 95
Sexually transmitted diseases (STDs), 101
Shepler, Susan, 81, 97
Sierra Leone: conflict profile, 173–174; critical moment of making decision/responding to crisis, 69; demobilization and reintegration, 99–100, 130; education/training/employment, 125; girls and boys, 86, 97, 99–100, 102; irrevocable nature of decision, not realizing, 111; leave, recruits not allowed to, 111; poverty, 41–42, 107; recruitment of young soldiers, 73; reflective thoughts of young soldier, 121; research and methodological issues, 141; volunteering concept, 107
Silence and the interview process, 154
Sinhala nationalism, 177–178. *See also* Sri Lanka
South Africa: adolescence, specific features of, 31–32; Bantu Education Act, 17; conflict profile, 175–176; critical moment of making decision/responding to crisis, 71; demobilization and reintegration, 131, 133; education/training/employment, 15–18, 20–21, 47; family/social support networks, 24, 51; girls and boys, 86, 88; military/parties to the conflict influencing youth involvement, 57; parental consent, 116; peer group influence, 26, 52; politics and ideology, 27, 59, 60; research and methodological issues, 143; role-models, soldiers/militants as, 92
Soviet Union and Afghanistan, 163
Sri Lanka: adolescence, specific features of, 29; conflict profile, 177–178; critical moment of making decision/responding to crisis, 70, 75; domestic exploitation/abuse, 88, 89;

economic motivations, 43–44; education/training/employment, 16, 22, 44, 46, 96; family/social support networks, 24, 48; girls and boys, 86, 96, 97; military/parties to the conflict influencing youth involvement, 11, 56; parental consent, 116; politics and ideology, 59, 60; poverty, 14; recruitment of young soldiers, 54–56, 72; research and methodological issues, 141; self-protection, feeling the need for, 40, 96; volunteering concept, 106

Strasser, Valentine, 173

Taliban, 163–164. *See also* Afghanistan

Tamil United Liberation Front (TULF). *See also* Sri Lanka

Therapeutic relationships and the interview process, 155–156

Thirty Years War (1618-1648), 81

Thompson, Carol, 101

Tradition/culture of violence/warfare, 31–36, 81, 86–87

Tutsi people, 169

Uganda, 169–170. *See also* Democratic Republic of Congo

UNICEF, 97

United Kingdom: adolescence, specific features of, 30; critical moment of making decision/responding to crisis, 68, 71; culture/tradition of violence/warfare, 32; economic motivations, 43; education/training/employment, 19–20, 22, 46, 47; family/social support networks, 51; girls and boys, 86; military environment, normality of the, 11; peer group influence, 52–54; recruitment of young soldiers, 54, 61–62; research and methodological issues, 37(note 3),140, 141; volunteering concept, 107–108 *See also* Ireland, Northern

United Nations, 137, 174

UN Study on the Impact of Armed Conflict on Children, 3

van Holde, Stephen, 81

Violent behavior legitimized by living in context of armed violence, 12–13

Volunteering, the concept of: conclusions/summary, 117; education/training/employment, 107–108; family/social support networks, 107; 15 as cutoff age for consent, 113, 117; forced *vs.* not forced, 83, 105–107, 112; irrevocable nature of the decision, not realizing, 110–111; leave, recruits not allowed to, 110, 111, 128–129; legal issues, 112–117; options, joining armed groups because of lack of other, 108; parental consent, 116; reality of what they are getting into, not knowing, 108–109

War as environmental factor leading to young soldiers: escape from home, war offering an, 13–14; family/social support networks disrupted, 13; guns, availability/familiarity with, 13; insecurity created at several levels, 39–41; military environment, normality of the, 10–12; options, joining armed groups because of lack of other, 41; overview, 9–10; risk factors common to young soldiers linked, 80; self-protection, feeling the need for, 13, 40–41; summary identifying it as key factor in research, 124–125; violent behavior legitimized by living in context of armed conflict, 12–13. *See also* Factors making young people vulnerable to military participation

Wessells, Michael, 79

Worst Forms of Child Labour Convention No. 182 (1999), 113, 114

Yhombi-Opango, Jacques-Joachim, 167

Young soldiers. *See* Factors making young people vulnerable to military participation; *individual subject headings*

Yugoslavia and girls and boys, 98

Zimbabwe, cleansing child soldiers in, 101

About the Book

They are part of rebel factions, national armies, paramilitaries, and other armed groups and entrenched in some of the most violent conflicts around the globe. They are in some ways still children—yet, from Afghanistan to Sierra Leone to Northern Ireland, you can find them among the fighters. Why?

Young Soldiers explores the reasons that adolescents who are neither physically forced nor abducted choose to join armed groups. Drawing on in-depth interviews with the soldiers themselves, the authors challenge conventional wisdom to offer a thought-provoking account of the role that war, poverty, education, politics, identity, family, and friends all play in driving these young men and women to join military life. They also address the important issues of demobilization and the reintegration process.

International in scope, covering a variety of situations in Afghanistan, Colombia, Congo-Brazzaville, Democratic Republic of Congo, Pakistan, Sierra Leone, South Africa, Sri Lanka, and the United Kingdom, *Young Soldiers* concludes with a discussion of the steps needed to create an environment in which adolescents are no longer "forced" to volunteer.

Rachel Brett is representative for human rights and refugees at the Quaker United Nations Office in Geneva. She is also a fellow of the Human Rights Centre at Essex University. **Irma Specht** is an anthropologist and director of the consultancy firm Transition International. She was for many years responsible for International Labour Organization program development, research, and policy issues concerning the reintegration of excombatants.